Robert Fleming Sample

Memoir of the Reverend John C. Thom

Robert Fleming Sample

Memoir of the Reverend John C. Thom

ISBN/EAN: 9783337400453

Printed in Europe, USA, Canada, Australia, Japan

Cover: Foto ©Lupo / pixelio.de

More available books at **www.hansebooks.com**

MEMOIR

OF THE

REV. JOHN C. THOM.

BY THE

REV. ROBERT F. SAMPLE.

WITH AN INTRODUCTION,

BY THE

REV. W. S. PLUMER, D. D.

PHILADELPHIA:

JAMES S. CLAXTON,

SUCCESSOR TO WM. S. & ALFRED MARTIEN.

1214 Chestnut Street.

1868.

Entered, according to the Act of Congress, in the year 1867,
By Rev. ROBERT F. SAMPLE,
In the office of the Clerk of the District Court for the Eastern District of Pennsylvania.

PRINTED BY ALFRED MARTIEN.

CONTENTS.

	Page
INTRODUCTION	5

CHAPTER I.
Birth—Childhood—Religious Experience—Enters the Academy.. 13

CHAPTER II.
Enters Jefferson College—Revival—Afflictions—Graduation... 30

CHAPTER III.
Returns to Eldersridge—The Teacher—The tender Nurse—Efforts to do good... 48

CHAPTER IV.
Teaches in Natchez, Mississippi—The Pestilence—Diligence, and Success—Pleasant Relations—Returns North.. 58

CHAPTER V.
Extracts from Journal... 70

CHAPTER VI.
Enters Theological Seminary at Princeton—Attentive to duty—Growth in Piety—Licensure—Called to Waynesburg, Pennsylvania.................................... 100

CHAPTER VII.

Enters upon his labors in Waynesburg—Ordained and installed—The Earnest Preacher, and Faithful Pastor—Revival—Attention to the bereaved, the poor, the stranger, the aged, and the young 117

CHAPTER VIII.

Benevolence urged—Co-operation on the part of the Church—Habits of Study—Style of preaching—Jesus only.. 141

CHAPTER IX.

Characteristics—Self-forgetfulness—Patience—Hospitality—Sympathy—Concern for souls—Cheerfulness—Depression.. 166

CHAPTER X.

The Husband and Father... 179

CHAPTER XI.

Miscellaneous Letters.. 189

CHAPTER XII.

Afflictions—Visits army—Labors in other churches—Invasion of Pennsylvania by the Confederates—Enters the army as a private—Chosen Chaplain—Faithful labor, and its results—Returns home....... 203

CHAPTER XIII.

Last days at Waynesburg—Called to St. Louis—Sad partings.. 222

CHAPTER XIV.

Labors in the Pine Street Church of St. Louis—Recalled to Pennsylvania by domestic affliction—Returns to St. Louis—Sickness—Death..................... 237

INTRODUCTION.

The memoirs of even bad men may be useful in warning us against their errors and their doom. So mankind generally judge. So inspired writers have decided, by sketching the history of not a few, who were a curse and not a blessing. Much more may the biography of good men be profitable in instructing us in a way that is good, and in inciting us to seek for glory, honor, and immortality.

The subject of the following memoir was a very good man. Perhaps no one, who knew him, will hesitate to give a hearty assent to this statement. Nor should his early death hinder the publication of his memoir. Some men die old in experience and usefulness at thirty years of age; while others, who live twice as long, seem to have lived in vain. He has lived long, who has glorified God in the earth, and finished the work God gave him to do. Mr. Thom was a man remarkable for his humility, cheerfulness, deep experience, reliance on the promises, conscientiousness, industry, and usefulness. He lived a great deal in a short time. Nor does it detract from his credit or the probable utility of his record, that he spent most of his ministerial life in comparative privacy. I have seen him in the midst of his plain, worthy, and intelligent people, moving noiselessly, always commanding respect, constantly watching for opportunities to speak a word in season, and often making a deep impression by a single sentence. I did not therefore wonder at the happy influence which he everywhere exerted.

It seems to be generally agreed that well written memoirs of persons venerable for years, piety, and services, are entitled to much favor. Of late years, also, the public have received with much kindness sketches of the lives of young children. Surely, then, the biography of those who are cut down in the midst of their days and of their usefulness cannot be destitute of interest or instruction.

Sometimes, when we read the lives of very great men, we are filled with wonder at their prodigious powers, and at the amazing results of their plans and labors. There never was but one Gustavus Adolphus, one Turenne, one Washington, one Paul, one Bunyan, one Whitefield. When we read to what they rose, we say, It is high, we cannot attain to it. But when we behold the struggles, conflicts, and successes of such a man as dear Mr. Thom, many an humble and good man, possessed of good sense, a ready perception of plain truth, and a fair opportunity of cultivating his mind, heart, and manners, says, By God's grace I too may be a blessing to the world; I too may rise to honor; I too may shine as the stars for ever and ever.

I have not seen the biography contained in this volume. I have merely seen the table of contents. But even without perusal, I cannot hesitate to commend it to the reader. The author is one whom I have long esteemed.

He is very capable of doing his work well. In his labor he has been animated by a strong and tender love to the memory of the departed. And in the life of Mr. Thom he could not have failed to find much that was worthy of statement or delineation. He has also had access to the best sources of information.

If any inquire for the secret of Mr. Thom's usefulness, the answer should point immediately to the grace of God, which toward him was very abundant. To the power of the Holy Spirit both he and his best friends ascribed all that was above and beyond unregenerate human nature.

While this is unquestionable, we still look at particular points in Mr. Thom's character, which were employed by the God of all grace for making him a chosen vessel for conveying spiritual good to many. He had an uncommon measure of that uncommon quality—common sense. This was the means of preserving him from a thousand follies, which destroy or impair usefulness. It kept him from wild fancies and vagaries, in which so many bury their opportunities of doing good. He was not carried away by mere plausibilities. He attempted no impossible things. He took men as he found them. He did not heal slightly the hurt of God's people. He cast not pearls before swine, nor gave that which is holy unto the dogs. He discerned both time and judgment. He did not put new wine into old bottles.

Then, he was humble, and so free from the arrogance of pride, justly offensive to men. It was easy for him in honor to prefer others. He loved to learn from any who could give him either instruction or information. He abhorred vain pretensions. He readily condescended to men of low estate. He was habitually ready to receive the decisions of God's word on all points of faith and practice. Even his prudential maxims were chiefly drawn from Scripture, especially the book of Proverbs.

Another thing prominent in Mr. Thom's character was benevolence. He loved sincerely and ardently. Very tenderly did he pity both the sorrowing and the sinful. Who ever heard him, in all his public life, say a word that could be fairly construed into malevolence? He prayed for his enemies. He blessed, and cursed not. He abhorred all double-dealing, all calumny, all evil surmising. He forgave as he hoped to be forgiven.

And his zeal abounded. He was, upon deep conviction, a staunch and uniform friend of pure, solemn, powerful revivals of religion. He never doubted the wisdom of God in granting harvests both to the husbandman and to him who gathereth fruit unto life eternal. In his early years he witnessed some of the most remarkable displays of Divine grace in the conversion of many souls. The memory of these, confirmed by Scripture, was hallowed, even as the scénes of Bethel doubtless always lingered about the mind of Jacob. He had seen God's power and glory.

But Mr. Thom early settled in his mind that pure revivals of religion were not to be expected except in connection with sound religious instruction. Therefore he was diligent in teaching the people knowledge. He desired.

that the word of God might dwell in them richly in all wisdom and spiritual understanding. To this end he was instant in season and out of season. I think he excelled most men in remembering that the night cometh when no man can work, and that he which converteth the sinner from the error of his way shall save a soul from death, and shall hide a multitude of sins.

The life and labors of such a man, when known, must be useful to many. In his early removal from the church below, many mourn. But the death of every believer is in answer to the intercession of our Lord Jesus Christ: "Father, I will that they also, whom thou hast given me, be with me where I am; that they may behold my glory, which thou hast given me." John xvii. 24. It often happens that "God takes them soonest, whom he loves best." The memory of Mr. Thom is precious to thousands. In his death I mourn the loss of one of the best and most unflinching friends, and one of the most modest, manly, and agreeable companions of my life. For this Memoir

I bespeak the most friendly regards of my acquaintance; and for the amiable and desolate widow of the deceased, and for his fatherless and promising children, I bespeak all the good will due to those whose father and husband lived to show kindness and do good to all men as he had opportunity.

WM. S. PLUMER.

Theological Seminary, Columbia, S. C.
September 25, 1867.

MEMOIR

OF THE

REV. JOHN C. THOM.

CHAPTER I.

BIRTH—CHILDHOOD—ENTERS THE ACADEMY.

John Culbertson Thom was born in Clarion county, Pennsylvania, April 19th, 1830. His parents were of Scotch-Irish descent, and members of the Presbyterian Church. His grandfather came to this country when a boy, and participated in the struggle for American Independence. He lived for a time in Westmoreland county, Pennsylvania, where he married a sister of General A. Craig, of Revolutionary memory. John Thom, the father of John Culbertson, was brought up according to the old Presbyterian mode. When quite young he was a subject of the *falling exercise*, then prevailing in that region. He was a godly man, and possessed more than ordinary force of character. In 1812 he married Margaret Culbertson, whose father, a fine scholar, had educated her much beyond the average of that day. She was remarkably gentle, sensitive, retiring, and pious. She loved her home, and it was the sphere of her greatest usefulness. She drew largely from the resources of her youth in the education of her children, giving special attention to their religious culture; mingling sacred history, texts of Scripture, and pleasant poems in her daily teachings. She was spared to her family but a few years after the birth of her youngest child, "the Benjamin" of the household; but in that short period she had planted precious seed in the mind of her darling boy, whose heart seemed, in early childhood, to be turned toward heaven. She was an ardent lover of nature, and her refined taste reappeared in her son.

Much might be said of the educational influence of scenery. The natural surroundings of early life no doubt determine, to a considerable extent, the habits of thought and feeling through all the subsequent years. The life of which we write was associated in childhood with one of the sweetest spots in a region noted for its picturesque beauty. Our thoughts revert to an unpretending little house, nestling among the hills. There was a lawn and flower garden in front of it, a large orchard behind it. In summer the hills were clothed with all the varied tints of forest green, from the light poplar and quivering aspen tree, to the feathery pine and sombre hemlock, and through the shady valley near by, a little brook went softly murmuring on its way, while the over-hanging branches were gay with birds of tenderest note and fairest plumage, and the air was ladened with the fragrance of wild flowers.

The mother was wont to associate religion, in the minds of her children, with the beautiful surroundings of their home. When she told them the names of plants and flowers, marked their delicate tints and grateful fragrance, she directed their thoughts to Him who made the lilies, and "so clothed the grass of the fields." The sparkling waters, too, were associated with the streams which make glad the city of our God, and with the river of the water of life. When, wearied with play, the little ones gathered around her in the evening twilight, watching the stars as they came out from their chambers in the sky, and learning from her their names, she spoke of the "Morning Star," of the "Star of Bethlehem," and of them who, having turned many to righteousness, "shall shine as the stars for ever and ever." So that being dead, she yet spake to the bereaved family who now, indeed found

"Tongues in trees, books in the running brooks,
Sermons in stones, and good in everything."

Like all the children, the youngest was early taught the important duty of filial obedience. The word of the parent was law in the home, and loving submission was promptly yielded. One day John was sporting about the house in great glee, happy as a child could be. After awhile, becoming thirsty, he asked his mother for water. His father brought it, but he was unwilling to take it from any one except the mother, and persisted in the refusal. Then the father took the cup in one hand and a rod in the other, telling the child to drink. Still he would not. After a few strokes of the rod, the cup was again offered, and refused as before. But the will of the child must yield to the will of the parent, or sad consequences may follow. Nearly two hours elapsed before submission was secured. Then John put his arms about his father's neck and kissed him, and never again refused to obey a direct command.

John's love for his mother was very strong. In later years he clung to her memory with a beautiful and touching affection. He seemed to inherit the strong will of his father, and the tender sensibilities of his mother; a manly head and a womanly heart. His gentle mother died shortly before he attained to his fourth year—that tender mother whose touch had always soothed her boy, whose kind look had always comforted him. They buried her on a cold November day. Her bosom was his refuge no longer, and ever after the shadow of her grave rested on his heart.

On the evening of that sad funeral day, when sympathizing friends had all gone to their homes, and the little household, left alone in their great sorrow, gathered for family prayers, John sat in his accustomed place, silently looking at his father, who tried in vain to sing the evening hymn. Alas! the voice that had daily joined his in the sweet psalms of praise was hushed, and the children, however much they may have wished to aid their sorrow-stricken parent, could not do it. That evening John resolved that he would try to take his mother's place in this part of their devotions, and, though many difficulties surrounded him, his great motive so helped him, that when still a mere child he led the family singing. In after years he excelled in vocal music, and the writer has often been deeply moved whilst hearing him sing some touching hymn concerning Jesus, the resurrection, or heaven.

Soon after the death of his mother, John was taken sick. He grew worse day by day, pined away, and at length seemed to be on the borders of the grave. The father felt deeply anxious for his boy, and wrestled with God for his life. He prevailed; and receiving his child as one from the dead, dedicated him anew to God.

This was a sad and weary winter to John, who mourned much for his mother. But with returning spring he regained his wonted strength, and returned, with the happy elasticity of childhood, to his usual pastimes.

It had been a custom with the children, when the winter was past, to go into the woods near by and look for wild flowers, which very early lifted their petals among the dry leaves, and this season they went as usual, though there was no lap at home to receive their precious burdens when they returned. One morning in April, when thus engaged, their father being absent from home, they discovered that a small building adjoining the house was on fire. In a little while the flames communicated with the main building. Great was the alarm of the children, and they hastened home. John was a brave boy, but, too young to contend with the devouring element, his characteristic tenderness overcame every other feeling, and clinging to his eldest sister, he would not allow her to enter the burning dwelling. So the mother's silver, the father's library, and nearly all the household goods were destroyed. The sister wept, but John and the other children were very cheerful, when, at a distance, they watched the progress of the flames, and saw the leaves of burning books borne upward on the heated currents, falling by and by like silvery ashes all around. John insisted it did not matter much about the property when "the children were all safe and nobody hurt." In the evening, when Mr. Thom returned, he gathered his family into a room of the "old mill," and with his boy's loving arms about his neck, he thanked God that they still had so comfortable a home.

In the course of time Mr. Thom married

again. His second wife was a prudent, Christian woman. And although John revered the memory of his own maternal parent, he yielded such respect and obedience to his new mother, as bound them together in warm affection whilst life lasted. He would allow no disparaging remarks to be made concerning her. To his sister, when uttering some sentiment he did not quite approve, he would say, "Now stop, sister—you mustn't." She was worthy of his love, and very beautiful and touching were his tokens of remembrance in later years.

Mr. Thom, who had been engaged in manufacturing, subsequently removed to a pleasant farm which he owned, near by. This change gave full exercise to the active mind of John, who delighted in gathering in the lambs, tending the cattle, and making himself useful in many ways. An old man once remarked: "It is a great pity to send that boy to school, he would make such an excellent farmer!" Whatever he did was done with all his might. He entered with great zest into the innocent sports and recreations common among boys of his age, and in all his intercourse with his companions he manifested a spirit of rare generosity, and kind consideration for the feelings of others. Thus he spent his childhood, a truthful, loving boy; seldom in contact with the rough or profane, a stranger to the great world without, his little stores of knowledge chiefly obtained from nature, the family Bible, and the patient instructions of the Christian home.

On the 13th of June, 1846, in the seventeenth year of his age, he was admitted to full communion in the church at New Rehoboth, in Clarion Presbytery, under the pastoral care of Rev. James Montgomery, in which church his father had long been a ruling elder. He does not seem to have been the subject of any remarkable religious impressions at the time. It is probable that he was converted in early childhood, if not sanctified from his birth. There was a gradual unfolding of the divine life as he grew in years, and at length from a sense of duty, attracted also by the beauty of Immanuel, he made a public profession of faith in Christ. Soon after this he began the study of the Latin Grammar, preparatory to a thorough literary course, reciting for a time to his pastor, and for this purpose riding a distance of seven miles.

He was tenderly attached to his younger sisters, and they regretted his daily absence from home. One of these he would take with him on his horse, carrying her quite near to the village, hiding her among the bushes until his return, she remaining quite contentedly with the flowers and birds while he was occupied with his recitations. After spending some time with his pastor he entered the Academy in Clarion, then under the care of Mr. Robert Sutton, afterwards a minister in the Presbyterian Church. This was a happy season to the young student, and it was, perhaps, more noted for the expansion of his social qualities than progress in studies, though he ranked high in his classes. Still retaining the simplicity and warm sympathies of childhood, he attracted his younger associates in the school. Several of these would occasionally accompany him in his brief visits home, and then had what they called a "grand time," climbing the hills and gathering wild flowers, or rambling through the bending orchard, and feasting on the mellow fruit. Then, too, he secured the affections of young men, some of whom entered the ministry before him, whilst others have joined him in the Better Country.

Leaving the school in Clarion, he taught in a district near by, during the winter of 1848-9, and the following spring entered the Presbyterial Academy at Eldersridge, which was then, as it is now, under the superintendence of Rev. Alex. Donaldson, D. D. During his connection with this honored institution he habitually manifested a determination to be punctual in attendance upon all duty, and to be thoroughly prepared in every exercise. He made rapid advance in his studies, and was considered one of the most thorough students that had ever attended the Academy. He had a strong will, and whilst he studiously avoided infringing upon the rights of others, he resolutely maintained his own. On one occasion an altercation took place between him and an assistant teacher. The latter appealed for redress to the principal, and demanded a public apology from the young student. After a careful investigation of the case, it was discovered that the pupil was not in fault, and he gave evidence of so much conscientiousness, and dignity of character, as to make a most favorable impression on the principal, who did not even remotely hint at an apology such as had been demanded. Nearly ten years after this occurrence he stated that at that time he began to strive anew for the mastery over his spirit, and his success was most signal, for there have been but few whose self-control and patience in suffering were so great.

His health was quite precarious, and at the Academy he was deeply impressed at times with the conviction that his days would be few. This impression never entirely left him. In his journal, May 25th, 1851, after referring to a severe sickness, he asks for increase of grace. "Oh! that God would give me a stronger faith, and preparation for my change. Then would I gladly lie down and be at rest, for I feel that my home is not here."

He highly appreciated the religious privileges enjoyed at the Academy, as appears from the following:

"June 1. Attended church. Heard two very interesting discourses by Rev. Alex. Donaldson. Subject of the Lecture in the morning, 1 Peter iii., from the 16th verse to the close. In the afternoon, sermon on Isaiah xlix. 24, 25. Discussion singularly able, and application peculiarly solemn. How can we remain cold under such distinguished means of grace! Only the Spirit of God can awaken us. In the evening attended the students' Prayer-meeting; made some remarks on the causes of spiritual decline, and the means of revival. The meeting appeared solemn; but few in attendance. O, God, revive thy work!"

"June 5. Unwell. Pain in my head. Sister M— is ill. May these things teach us our frailty, and stir us up to make sure work for eternity."

"June 8. Feel better, but not entirely well. Went to class to-day, but came home before the exercises were concluded, that I might stay with a sick friend. Two at his house are quite ill. O, God, Thou art giving us line upon line, and precept upon precept, but still how little art Thou in all our thoughts!"

"June 19. Last evening attended prayer-meeting. Several ministers present. Earnest and stirring appeals were made, particularly by Mr. Donaldson, who spoke a few minutes on the danger of stopping short of entire surrender to Jesus, even when the kingdom of heaven comes nigh to us. With such appeals, if our hearts were not harder than adamant, they surely would melt."

"Sabbath. Was called upon to instruct a class of young ladies; had considerable freedom in imparting instruction. Endeavored to impress upon their minds the duty and necessity of following Christ. Was called upon to close the Sabbath-school with prayer; felt some liberty in addressing the throne of grace."

Many similar extracts might be made. But we must content ourselves with one or two more.

"June 22. Went last evening to see E— T—, thought to be in a dying condition. She is young, and surrounded with all the comforts wealth can purchase, yet appears in a delightful frame of mind in prospect of death: willing to go. Was much cheered by her godly conversation. May she be more and more purified, and may I be improved by the dispensations of Providence witnessed upon others."

June 23. Our Bible-class did not meet to-day, the teacher being absent. Felt drowsy and stupid part of the time, but had some seasons of sweet communion with God. Attended prayer-meeting this evening. Spoke a few minutes on the evidences of growing coldness among us. Felt some freedom in prayer. Oh! may I have more frequent and intimate communion with God, and feel more earnest desires after holiness."

During all his stay at Eldersridge he maintained a consistent Christian deportment, exerting a happy influence on his fellow-students, encouraging studiousness, good order, and respect for religion. He was absent one winter, teaching in the neighborhood of his home, but completed his academic course in September, 1851, leaving Eldersridge with pleasant memories, and much regret.

CHAPTER II.

STUDENT AT JEFFERSON COLLEGE.

In the autumn of 1851, Mr. Thom entered Jefferson College, at Canonsburg, Pennsylvania. That institution was then under the Presidency of Rev. A. B. Brown, D. D., a successful educator, an eloquent preacher, and one of the most lovely Christian characters of his day.

Mr. Thom was admitted to the Junior Class, in which he ranked among the highest, and in the Literary Society he had few, if any, superiors. His much loved friend and classmate, now the Hon. Thomas Ewing, of the Pittsburgh bar, gave the almost unanimous opinion of his fellow-students when he thus wrote of Mr. Thom: "He was industrious, energetic, and persevering; a man of more than ordinary talent and intellect. As a competitor in a long, steady, mental strife, I would have considered him the most dangerous opponent in our class. In the annual contest of 1853, he represented his society as essayist, and carried off the honor from a man who then, and now, ranks high in ability." His manner was not at all times pleasing. Some considered him haughty and proud. The opinion may have been correct, but, in the judgment of those who knew him best, it was considered erroneous, and the peculiar bearing which gave rise to this misapprehension was, in later years, to a considerable extent corrected. Some enemies he had, but no one ever charged him with neglect of duty, or with a violation of any principle of morality, or true manliness.

When he left Eldersridge, that institution and the church, both under the care of the Rev. Dr. Donaldson, were enjoying a precious revival of religion. The religious condition of the college was very different, and to him the contrast was painful. In his journal we find the following record:

"September 28th, 1851. Since I last wrote,

my situation has indeed been changed. I have left a place hallowed by many tender associations. But duty called, and I closed my career as a student in the academy for ever. Though kind friends now extend to me the sweet consolations of Christian sympathy and fellowship, it is but natural that the heart should turn with strong affection to scenes wrapt in the mists of the past. But shall I never enjoy similar pleasures? never again delight in those beatific joys which can only spring from communion with pious friends, and with God? or shall I never feel the gracious outpouring of the Spirit drawing me, with those I love, to Him, and hear many inquiring the way to Zion, weeping as they go?"

At this time he felt the need of special watchfulness, and realized his dependence upon God. Former restraints were to a great extent removed. Tender voices that once bid him stand fast in the truth, were indistinctly heard across the space that separated him from the scenes of earlier years, and unlooked for influences, unfavorable to religious growth, gathered about him. There is reason to believe that he lost much of the ardor and strength of Christian love, which had so marked a great deal of his experience at Eldersridge. This afterwards became a source of sorrow and deep humiliation. At one time he gives expression to his anxiety and hopes in language such as this: "Temptations of no ordinary nature surround me. I have taken another step out into the wide world, and henceforth the influence of home will be but feebly felt. If God spare my life, my course will still be onward. How shall the contest be sustained? I thank God for the hope of assistance through Jesus Christ my Lord. Were it not for *that*, my expectations would indeed be vain. And yet how cold is my heart! How few affections in heaven! How much my thoughts are engrossed with the cares and pleasures of this life! O, for a closer walk with God!"

"Sabbath. Heard a sermon to-day on the text: 'We are saved by hope;' in which the speaker alluded to the duty of making our calling and election sure. When shall I cease to be harassed with doubts? O God, remove these from my mind!"

Several miscellaneous extracts from his journal may be introduced in this connection. "Heard of the death of a dear friend, the mother of two dear ones (cousins), who are now without a parent on earth. O, were it not for the consolations of religion, how could such bereavements be endured?" One of these cousins, Lizzie Culbertson, afterwards spent several years as a missionary among the Choctaws, and is now the wife of Rev. Hunter Corbett, who is laboring in China.

"October 11. Spent the evening in company with some young persons who were previously strangers. In one of these the Christian graces seemed to be developed in an extraordinary degree. Spent some time in interesting, and I hope profitable, conversation; though, with shame and sorrow, I must confess that the greater part of the interview was characterized by forgetfulness of God.

"Heard this evening of the brutal assault of one student upon another, and serious injury inflicted. O, when shall the good hand of our God be upon us, to curb our evil passions, and lead us in the paths of true holiness!

"October 12. Dr. Brown being ill, there were no services in the chapel. Went to the Methodist church for the first time in many months. Thought the discourse was weak, yet it contained matter for reflection. May I have grace to improve it! Feel very deeply concerned for my room-mate who is, I fear, far from God. May I have grace to cast some influence around him that shall be blest to his soul. O, that God would arouse him from the lethargy of sin!

"October 18. Some young friends from Eldersridge, whom I have been expecting, came on to the Female Seminary to-day. Bereaved ones! May the arm of Omnipotence be underneath them; may his rod and staff guide and comfort them." Two of these friends were orphaned cousins, referred to in a previous extract from his journal. They were very lovely young ladies, and not far from the kingdom. Through the darkness of their great sorrow, God led them into the light of a good hope in Jesus. One of them is now in heaven. A third cousin was also an orphan. She afterwards married the Rev. W. S. Wilson, and a few years later, with a calm trust in Jesus, went to the heavenly home. With these orphans Mr. Thom sympathized with the tenderness of a brother, and helped them through many a dark passage in their seasons of affliction.

On the same day he writes: "Did not see Mr. B——. Felt very sorry, as he is one of the few in this cold world whose hearts are warm with love to God and man. In the evening Mrs. D—— handed me a beautifully bound copy of the life of Rev. Robert Murray McCheyne, with this inscription on the blank leaf,—'To Mr. J. C. Thom; a memento of obligation, and token of true regard, from his friends, Alex. Donaldson and John M. Barnet, Eldersridge, Pa., October 16, 1851.' O! how unworthy of such a token I feel myself to be. Never before did I realize so deeply how far short I came of doing my duty to those men whose kindness to me was very distinguished. And whilst I feel my unworthiness to receive this token from men, may I reflect how undeserved are the blessings of God, and may I more fully consecrate myself to his service, and live to his honor and glory." When it is borne in mind that Mr. Thom was quite young at this time, and had, with many others, simply sustained the relation of pupil to the friends who gave him this memento of affection, the high regard in which he was held will be more apparent.

"Oct. 19—Sabbath. Read in the Life of McCheyne. O, for the grace that characterized that young saint, so early called home... Heard Rev. Mr. Ewing preach an excellent sermon on the text: "A double minded man is unstable in all his ways."

"Dec. 14—Sabbath. Have to lament, as usual, my coldness and hardness of heart; also a disposition to feel complacency on account of the performance of external duty.

Trust I have in some measure enjoyed the presence of God. Felt encouraged and strengthened by conversation with a friend on some of the beauties of the Scriptures. Why do we not oftener speak together of the things of God? O, for more grace!"

About six months after Mr. Thom entered college, an extensive revival of religion occurred in the church connected with the college, and it extended throughout the village. In this work of grace he was greatly interested, and labored with much earnestness for the conversion of his irreligious companions. Some of these he visited in their rooms, with others he conversed as they walked by the way. To a few he wrote earnest appeals to be reconciled to God, accompanying the message with fervent prayer. Again he rejoiced in the dawning evidences of piety in the hearts of his fellow-students, and was himself elevated to a higher life. From his journal of March 21, 1852, we extract the following passage: "With a full heart I record what God has done for us. He has again visited us in mercy and not in wrath, and we trust many have been called from darkness to light. O! what a privilege, to pass through such scenes, when the Spirit descends with power, and sinners in Zion, as well as out of it, are made to tremble. I thank God that he has permitted me to see another time of refreshing from his presence. O! may it not be for my condemnation. I trust I feel, as I never felt before, our entire dependence on God. The work, O God, is thine. I feel also, I hope, more than ever the value and efficacy of prayer. May I always be importunate. I have had some precious evidence in the past few weeks of the readiness of God to answer prayer. I have attended religious meetings for the last three weeks, almost every night, during which time many, we trust, have been called from death to life. ... I thank God for what he has done for us, especially for the hopeful conversion of my room-mate, for whom I have long prayed. May God be ever with him, and make him a chosen vessel in his service."

He was much concerned for his Sabbath-school class, noting, with thankfulness and hope, indications of growing seriousness. And it was a matter of rejoicing to him, that all whom he made subjects of special effort and prayer were hopefully converted.

The influence of that precious season lingered with him throughout the remainder of his entire course. But during the last few months of his connection with the college, there were circumstances which diverted his attention somewhat from the paramount claims of religion. The excitement of a literary contest, and the strife for collegiate honors which culminates near the close of a college course, were not without their influence upon him; but the diversion was only for a season, and his heart returned with a warmer gush of affection to Him whose fellowship is more to be desired than all the world can bestow.

It was with emotions of no ordinary sorrow that the young student contemplated his departure from college. He had formed many attachments, and it was a sore trial to sunder all the ties that bound him to the hill country, and his associates in enjoyment and toil.

Now the great world is before him. His little bark has been passing year by year into the broader channels of life, and now the wide prospect which opens before him alternately excites ambition, and weighs down his spirit. There were voices bidding him seek self-aggrandizement, and rise high in the world, but the still small voice of the Spirit whispered, "Worship God, and rise to heaven!"

"I find myself," he writes, "after the usual ceremonies, invested with my degree, and am what the world calls 'an educated man.' How insignificant it all now appears, and how little do I now feel prepared for the great duties of life! But after all, the preparation which is most needed, is that of the heart, which comes from God alone. May His grace be sufficient for me!"

About the time of his graduation his health began to fail, and afflictions in his father's family seemed to make it necessary to modify his plans, and defer his entrance upon a course of theological study. This was a great trial. The way seemed long and dark before him, but on the threshold of a sad and weary experience he knelt at the footstool of his unerring Father, saying, "My heart, cease thy wild throbbings; look up to God and say, 'Thy will be done.'" Then, with a stronger faith in Him who led Joseph like a flock, he rose, and went calmly on his way.

There is no part of our Father's discipline which is unnecessary. As in the physical, so in the moral kingdom, all the appointments of God are important, and subserve desirable ends. In the human frame there is not a bone, muscle, or nerve, which is useless,— without which the body would not lack something of its present symmetry and power. So in every plant there is not a leaf nor fibre, not a cell nor fluid, which does not answer some important purpose. In all the range of nature, in what is great and small, in all that is beautiful, grand, or comparatively insignificant, each element has its uses, and all combined, form a perfect unity.

So it is in the moral world. In all Christian experience there is no trial, disappointment, or suffering which is not necessary. Without affliction the spiritual nature would not attain to that fulness and beauty which God designs; without it the Christian would not be fitted for that particular sphere in heaven which God would have him occupy. "It is for your profit," is the voice of the rod, and faith responds, "It is the Lord, let Him do what seemeth Him good."

Mr. Thom's life was one of no ordinary affliction. His sensitive nature was peculiarly susceptible to suffering. His strong attachments to his family and friends made him a constant bearer of their sorrows. The heavy pecuniary losses sustained by his father, severe trials in which the family became involved, and his own ill health, accompanied with alarming symptoms, which made it doubtful whether he would ever be able to fulfil the cherished plans of his life—all these weighed heavily upon him. He seldom spoke of domestic and personal afflictions to any outside of the little home circle, but bore them with all the patience he could command, and resolutely addressed himself to the duty which God assigned. At times his cross seemed too heavy, and his submission failed. Hard thoughts of God would now and then intrude, and he would drift away from his anchorage. A feeling of resentment toward those who had wronged him and his, would gain the ascendency, and many a hard contest was waged on the silent battle-field of his soul, of which only his nearest friends knew anything, and they but in part.

But his afflictions were for his good. He felt that they were necessary, and his friends discerned more readily than himself the good resulting from them. He grew in the graces of the Spirit. Humility was deepened, faith was strengthened, and the tender sympathies of his nature, which so distinguished him, were gradually unfolded.

"Is this the way, my Father?—'Tis, my child,
　Thou must pass through the tangled, dreary wild,
　If thou wouldst reach the city undefiled,—
　　Thy peaceful home above.

"O Father, I'm weary!—Child, lean thy head
　Upon my breast; it was my love that spread
　Thy rugged path; hope on still, till I have said,
　　'Rest,—rest for aye above.'"

There is beauty and plaintiveness in a paragraph which we here transcribe from the journal. "The sweet breath of summer fans my aching brow. The mocking bird and robin praise the Giver of their being with all the glad exhilaration of life unknown to care. Bright, blessed beings, they flutter out their inch of life, and are seen no more! No shadows come across their unruffled happiness, and the dreams that vex man's troubled being come not to them. How then are we so much better than they? God cares for them as for us. 'One of them shall not fall on the ground without your Father.' No stain of sin destroys the lustre of their beauty, or the melody of their songs. No forebodings of an unknown evil disturbs their rest. In happy unconsciousness they sing, and love, and die! But we voyagers on a gloomy river that leads to an unknown sea, are tortured with spectres of the past, and frightened with visions of the future. From whence, and what are we; and whither are we borne? Through what unknown and untried changes must we pass, and where is the goal? Will endless cycles roll away and find us still the same sentient and imperfect beings, without the key to unlock the mysteries of our being, and with feeling enough to be conscious of our impotence? or shall we at last sink into happy unconsciousness of our littleness, and cease to beat the bars of our cage because they are contracted till they allow no room to flutter or to feel? Can we be happy in ignorance of all the future while our restless, inquiring minds remain? Could we endure the eternal routine of any life, if spread out before us for our contemplation?

"The sun rises higher. The morning carol

is over. The dreams of youth yield to the reflection of manhood, and the rhapsodies of philosophy to the simplicity of faith. Like an opium eater's dream, our troubled existence here will soon be over. 'After life's fitful fever we shall sleep well,' if the hand of our Father arrange the pillow for our head. And where now is my hope? 'In hoc vinces.'" (By this thou shalt conquer.)

CHAPTER III.

TEACHES AT ELDERSRIDGE, PENNSYLVANIA.

AFTER graduating with honor, in August, 1853, Mr. Thom left Canonsburg, and immediately returned to Eldersridge, as assistant teacher in the Presbyterial Academy. This position he held for two years, faithful to duty, highly esteemed and much beloved by the Principal, the students, and the people generally.

He was active in every good work. He did not confine himself to the labors of the academy, but rendered valuable aid to the pastor of the church, and devoted himself to the interests of the community in which his lot was cast.

Near the close of the first year of his tutorship, typhoid fever prevailed as an epidemic in the neighborhood of Eldersridge, and whilst many were unwilling to administer to the necessities of the sick and dying, he visited them promptly, unhesitatingly doing what he could to alleviate suffering. His patient attentions and pious counsels did much to facilitate recovery in those who survived, and to light up the dark valley to such as were called to pass through it.

"It is less than one little week," he writes to a friend, "since I last addressed you, and yet what a world of events have been crowded into those few days. Two more have gone to swell the pale host! When I wrote you last I was sitting at the bedside of Mr. B——. After watching till morning, I rode to Saltzburg, (a village seven miles distant,) for medicine, and on my way back met a rider who told me to hasten my return. When I entered Mr. B's room I found him apparently dying. I was weary with watching, but I could get no one to take my place, and through the whole day I sat, and marked the life-tide ebbing away. In the evening he died. With my own hands I composed his stiffening limbs for their last resting-place, arranged upon his already decomposing body the habiliments of the grave, assisted in bearing him to the burial-ground, lowered his remains into their narrow home, and heaped his kindred dust upon him."

Then others required attention, and soon intelligence comes that Mrs. I—— is dead. He went to the designated place. There he found a man or two of the neighborhood, but no female, except the grey-headed mother of the deceased, alone with her dead. In an adjoining room the husband, prostrated with the epidemic fever, just learning of his wife's death, was weeping aloud. Mr. Thom bathed the head of the sufferer, and soothed him as best he could. But there were other calls, and this faithful nurse must answer them. He left the house quietly, and walked sadly away—above him the broad arch of heaven, with its beautiful stars, and masses of thick, black clouds rolling along on the night wind.

Again he writes from the couch of a fever patient: "You speak of Mr. S——'s sermon, and wish I had heard it. I wish so, too, for I need my languishing graces revived. But I have had preaching of the most solemn and impressive kind. The skeleton preacher has been speaking—how eloquently! of the world to come. He who can look with stolid indifference upon a fellow-being, making his trembling approach to the bar of God, would probably not be moved by mortal oratory. I trust I have not listened altogether in vain. But alas! how much there is to be done! I am amazed at the hardness of my heart, and mourn that I have no more of the Spirit of Christ.

"Earthly ties are broken: earthly friends go to their long home. Here, indeed, the mourners go about the streets. Sorrow and sighing are our heritage. But there is an eternal citizenship in heaven; an immortality in the family of God. There, a Father's arm around us, a Father's hand shall wipe away all tears from all faces. O, let us go to Him with hearts overflowing with love!

"The epidemic seems to be abating, but we

thought so once before. We are in the hands of the Lord. Let Him do what seemeth good in His sight."

The panic occasioned by this single outbreak of disease greatly reduced the number of students. It would have been to Mr. Thom's interest to have accepted any of the calls by which he was urged to go into a much more lucrative connection with other schools. But out of sympathy with the academy in its troubles, he remained a year longer, aiding much in recruiting its numbers, and in establishing its reputation for thorough instruction.

This is only one of many incidents which might be cited, of what he was willing to sacrifice for the good of others, and the cause of Christ. And yet he guarded against an over-estimate of his labors and self-denials. He continued at his post "in weakness, anxiety, and frequent depression, lamenting, with shame and confusion of face, unfaithfulness to the students and to God."

At one period he complains of great coldness: "I do not know that I ever endured so long a season of spiritual depression. Now, indeed, God seems to be coming near, and offering to be gracious."

Writing to one of his regular correspondents just before a communion Sabbath, he says: "I had a letter to-day from a dear friend of former days, asking, in the most earnest manner, how to become a Christian. I think I never felt so much as now the weakness of man, and the awful responsibility resting on the professing Christian. May God give me wisdom! Rev. Mr. McElwain came to-day, and preached two most searching sermons. He talks to men as if he meant to be understood."

"Monday. Communion is now over. It was a sweet and solemn time. I hope there are good things in store for us. Surely the Lord hath spoken good concerning Israel. O, that we were able to get nearer to God!"

Not long after, he mentions an interesting fact: "Meetings for prayer and conference have been held in my room every night for the last week, but O, how dead we are! Spirit of the living God, come and breathe upon these dry bones, and they shall live!"

It was not long until God heard the cries of his people, and again opened windows in heaven over an institution and church which have been often and remarkably blessed, with "seasons of refreshing from the presence of the Lord."

The pastor labored with great earnestness, sustained by the prayers and coöperation of believers, and rejoiced in the precious harvest of souls. Mr. Thom spent days in fasting, and nights in prayer, whilst attending to his onerous duties in the Academy, and riding to Lebanon (four miles distant) to conduct an evening prayer-meeting.

He also addressed letters to unconverted friends, urging them to come to Jesus, and to come without delay. Thus he writes to one: "Will you be angry with me for addressing you this morning in the name of God? Will you despise the message, because brought by one sold under sin? I am concerned for your soul. Another time of solemn interest is passing, and faith almost fails." Then, with a peculiar sweetness, and touching references to the personal history of his unconverted friend, he pleads *for* Jesus and *with* Him, that unbelief may be laid down at the foot of the cross.

Then, too, he found time to write or speak encouragingly to God's people, urging them to plead for the conversion of their friends, "for His own name's sake," and when praying for their children, he reminded Him of His covenant. To one who mourned the death of a father he found time to address words of comfort, and the letter is so characteristic that we insert it here. "I am becoming familiar with scenes of death—the countenance ghastly and livid—the body cadaverous and ulcerated—the eye now wandering with vacant look, and now lit up with unwonted fire—the limbs stiffening for their last repose—the breath coming in short and painful gasps—the death rattle, the quivering flesh, the solemn stillness that tells all is over—the wail of the bereaved as the feelings so long strung to their utmost ten-sion suddenly relax, and the cold iron of despair enters the soul! Ah! I see it all. But no death scene is more vividly before me than that which I never saw, except through the medium of your bereaved and wounded heart. It may seem unkind to call up, and dwell upon, a topic fraught with such painful memories. I think otherwise. Sad as those memories are, there is pleasure in them still. It is sweet to think of the love we have enjoyed, though it be lost to us for ever. It is pleasant to meditate upon the infinite gain of our dear departed, though it cost us bitter, burning tears. It is elevating and purifying to realize that we have an earthly link binding us to the world of spirits, another dear one in our Father's house. And apart from all this, it is good sometimes to meditate upon the awful circumstances of dissolution, and the still more stupendous realities which ensue. It assists us to number our days, that we may apply our hearts to wisdom."

But we cannot tarry here. Much might be written of his faithfulness in his relations to the Academy, and the people with whom he associated in acts of worship and the pleasant amenities of social life. From what has already been noted, we learn the secrets of his power. It was no wonder that his influence over the students was great, and that the events of those two years, and especially those months of tribulation and subsequent revival, are remembered with emotions of mingled sorrow and gratitude by many to whom he ministered, who are now scattered over half a continent.

CHAPTER IV.

TEACHER IN NATCHEZ, MISSISSIPPI.

AFTER teaching two years at Eldersridge, a dear friend who was engaged in the same vocation in Natchez, Mississippi, earnestly solicited him to remove to that city, which, after much thought and prayer, he consented to do. Having devoted the most of the proceeds of his labors to his now dependent friends—his father having lost an arm, and being otherwise afflicted—and it being impracticable for him to enter the Theological Seminary, which he so much longed to do, he felt that duty called him to a field of labor where his pecuniary remuneration would be larger, and he might discharge at once the obligations of filial duty, and secure the means to continue his studies with reference to the ministry. Then, though the tender attachment of his friends led them to put every possible barrier in his way, and his naturally affectionate temperament made it hard for him to go, yet he broke away from all the ties of home and endeared friendship, and with "his whole being quivering with intense feeling" went forth to do, so far as he could, the work to which he felt God had called him.

On his journey southward he saw much to interest him, and discovered beauty where others looked for it in vain. Passing down the dull channel of the Mississippi he was charmed with the scenery along the route. The broad river, the beautiful islands, the autumn-tinted foliage, furnished entertainment, and suggested pleasant thoughts of Him who spread the "beautiful earth abroad."

His entrance into Natchez made a pleasant impression on his mind, and was long after recalled as one of the fairest pictures which memory had preserved. He enjoyed the ride through groves of honey-locusts, and magnolias, and yellow poplar, festooned with hanging moss, and wreathed with grape and muscatine vines, and through gardens adorned with banana and palm trees, growing with a luxuriance of which our northern imaginations can scarcely form a conception. "The situation of upper Natchez," he writes, "is exceedingly beautiful. It seems to me like a fairy land, even yet, in September, all blooming with roses. The streets are wide and shady, the grounds adorned with art and nature in perfection blended; the air is soft and fragrant; 'the tree top't mounds with spiral pathways, fringed with flowers;' the curiously trimmed evergreens, the orange groves and magnolias, the juicy pomegranates and blooming hedges, the park and the broad smooth river,—all unite in making this a place of wondrous beauty."

Though young, enthusiastic, and of a poetical turn of mind, he was no visionary. He entered with zeal upon the most practical duties, and was as persevering as he was diligent. He was engaged in the City Institute as principal of the senior department, also in a Female Seminary, and elsewhere; teaching, much of the time, nine hours and a half a day. In the Institute he taught Latin, Greek, and the higher Mathematics, and during the two years of his connection with the school he was absent from his duties but one day. Though his labors as instructor were very great, yet he was so methodical that he found time for miscellaneous reading, theological studies, writing, and social visiting, not neglecting any religious duty. He very soon formed a large circle of acquaintances, who did whatever could be done to make his sojourn pleasant.

Though he had many religious advantages in Natchez, yet he was peculiarly exposed to temptation, and associated with evil; but he maintained his Christian integrity—stood fast in the Lord. One who knew him intimately, a man of much intelligence, discernment, and piety, says of him: "From my first acquaintance with Mr. Thom, his religion was undoubted. Of it he made no ostentatious display, but it manifested its controlling influence over him on all occasions—in all circumstances. I never knew a more uniformly consistent Christian."

Not long after he commenced his labors in Natchez, the city was visited with that most dreadful of southern epidemics, the yellow fever. There was great consternation among the people generally. Strangers were more alarmed than the citizens, for they were in greater danger. With the other northern teachers, Mr. Thom was sent into the country, where it was supposed they would be comparatively safe. They were most kindly received to the home of an estimable widow lady, and remained there six weeks. Here Mr. Thom and his companions passed their time very happily, though soberly, as the epidemic passed around them. Their friendship grew stronger as the weeks advanced, and they drew nearer to God, whose protecting hand kept them from the "noisome pestilence."

Speaking of his isolation, and occasional loneliness, he writes: "My port-folio is my relief in depression. Thinking is my only relief from thought, and I never can think so obliviously as when I have pen and paper before me. I do not feel alarmed—not the least. I am in the hands of that God who has led me hitherto, and who, I am fully persuaded, will take care of me in the future. I never could say more truly than at this moment, 'Let Him do with me as seemeth Him good.'"

At a later period: "I think now that we are perfectly safe in the country, even if a few more cases should occur in the city. And, indeed, the mercy of God has been very specially manifested to us, for this is the only house in the neighborhood I know of, which has entirely escaped. And although I felt secure all the time, now I know there was but a step between me and death. Doubtless dear ones prayed for me, that the good hand of the Lord might be upon me."

He spoke in the highest terms of the Christian hospitality, and the motherly kindness of the lady who had so promptly received him, with others, to her palatial residence, and said, "this house seems a 'Bethel.' "

"I am not superstitious," he writes, "but I cannot help feeling sometimes that the mind looks forward, and takes its tone from the future. Especially did I think of this when I saw men around me, with no more liklihood of sickness than I, making their wills, and settling their business, preparatory to setting out to the undiscovered country. But I never felt any anxiety. I never could feel that I was in danger."

When the pestilence had passed by, Mr. Thom returned to the city, and resumed his duties in the Institute and Seminary. Teaching all day prepared him to enjoy the evening air, ladened with fragrance, sweeping up fresh and cool from the broad waters. The pleasant walks along the bluffs, and about the spacious gardens, would have lured out one more sedentary. Sometimes he watched with the sick. Occasionally he met with a Literary Society, and now and then he turned aside, in his twilight rambles, to listen to the apparently earnest devotions of the colored people who met, from time to time, to worship God in their untutored way.

He had a happy faculty of talking with young persons on religious subjects. Several of his pupils came to him with burdened hearts, asking for his counsel and prayers. Young hearts were laid bare to him in sorrow and contrition, which had been judged harshly by the world, but were susceptible of deep impressions from Divine truth, and were turning toward the cross. One day there came to him a lad, noted among his companions for a reckless way, that left the impression that he was peculiarly depraved. But as he talked to his teacher of his hopes and fears; of his mother whose home, now in heaven, he wished to share; of his tender remembrance of her care and her prayers, Mr. Thom felt hopeful, and encouraged him to follow on to seek the Lord. Afterward, the young wanderer seemed to enter the way of life, and invoked blessings on the head of him who helped him in his search for Jesus.

At the expiration of his first year in Natchez, he wrote thus in his diary: "August 30, 1856. One year of southern life is ended. Through all the dangers of a journey of many hundred miles, and the more alarming dangers of a fearful epidemic, Thy protection, O God, has been over me; and, sinful as I am, I trust a small measure of Thy grace is in my heart. I have suffered, but not as I deserved. I have been chastened, but gently. Enable me to record Thy goodness, and to adorn my Christian profession, not only here, but through my whole life.

"And now I am about to enter upon the arduous labors of another year. Do Thou help me. Aid me in my preparations for the gospel ministry, and give me grace to discharge the duties of that high calling, or keep me from profaning it. May God in mercy watch over me. I have no strength but His. May the blessing of God rest upon this household—(Mrs. North's.) May they never have occasion to regret their kindness to me, and may I prove a blessing to them, and the interesting pupils under my care."

Near the close of his second year, he announced his determination to return north, and devote all his time to preparation for the ministry. Many and strenuous efforts were made, with the view of inducing him to change his purpose. A large increase of salary was proposed. Parents and pupils besought him to stay. But he felt conscientiously constrained to adhere to his original plans.

Before leaving Natchez he received many pleasant tokens of affection, and expressions of gratitude for his labors. The lady in whose family he taught a portion of every day, was accustomed to call him her "child," and when he referred to his great indebtedness to her for her sympathy, and tender care of the stranger, she told him she was abundantly recompensed for it already, and that if it should ever be her privilege to hear him preach sweet messages of salvation, she would be recompensed a thousand-fold for all her care. On New-Year's day she presented him with a beautiful gold watch. He wrote an acknowledgment which deeply moved the feelings of the kind lady, and she replied in the following unique letter: "To prepare a New-Year's gift for you, my child, seems nothing strange to me, nor took a thought from my occupations. But your note! I have tried to read it without shedding tears, but each time I weep the same. I did not want you to think so much about it. Well, never mind, my child, some of these days you will graduate at the Seminary. You will soon stand in the sanctuary. Old and young will turn rapt faces to yours, as if they were looking up to heaven. You will point to the downward path that all most follow, and mingle dust with the dust of ages. You will then turn, beautifully and eloquently, to the new generation, and the life of the Spirit above, eternally with the Father of all. They will listen, and in their hearts all will call you blessed. By-and-by an old lady, journeying eastward, will stop at your 'village,' and attend church. She seats herself; wipes her glasses; adjusts the focus; surveys the church and people. The pastor rises. Lo! it is her own child. She suppresses, for some time, her emotions, but nature finally breaks away in a great sob. The people stare at the lady. The minister looks at the time, and perceives it is the precise time of the 'Old Lady's Recompense.'

'Dost like the picture.'"

But time passes. Tender ties must be sundered. Sad farewells must be spoken. With all the intoxication of success, all the flatteries of a highly appreciative people, all the tenderness of new friendships to detain him, he turned his back upon the south, his face towards the scenes of his childhood, and almost with a shout, with a fulness of feeling that few natures can appreciate, he hastened to his far off home, and toward the fulfilment of the cherished purpose of his life.

CHAPTER V.

EXTRACTS FROM JOURNAL.

IN his journal, kept at Natchez, in connection with the record of current events, he frequently expanded some thought suggested by his reading, or the occurrences of the day. Many of these effusions, though hastily written, are worthy of preservation. They indicate an amount of general information unusual in so young a man, and give us an insight into the inner life of the writer. Without further introduction we will here insert a few selections from these "Notes by the Way."

"February 15. The church bells peal the hour of worship. Sweetly solemn, their mingled voices fall on the stillness of the Sabbath, telling us that our merciful Father has brought us safely through another week, and now calls upon us to offer up our sacrifice of praise for His goodness; telling us, too, that we poor pilgrims here are not orphans also, tossed upon this troubled scene without a guardian or a guide, but the great ear is open to our cry, and the eye of infinite compassion looks upon us; telling us that there is still a link between us and the great world above, and leading us away from the sordid pursuits of this fleeting existence towards the great future; speaking of that most sublime circumstance, 'man in audience with the Deity.' But there is a tone of sadness in them too. Coming upon the breath of morning, they sound mournfully; like a funeral knell they speak of the grave, and all its melancholy associations; they speak of the loved and lost, with whom we took sweet counsel and walked to the house of God. But most of all, they speak of sin. Sad heritage; possession sadder still.

'E'en the rapture of pardon is mingled with fears,
And the cup of thanksgiving with penitent tears.'

"As the most impressive expression of sin ever made, or ever to be made, was the sacrifice of Christ, so, oft as the day returns it brings back the memory of our mournful condition. Away, away from the presence of our Father, exposed to the attacks and influences of malicious natures, and malicious spirits, like half-clad and houseless wanderers in a winter storm, we crouch and cower under the nearest shelter, and stand, shivering, as the storms of life roll on, instead of pressing vigorously onward toward our home, and the comfortable presence of God. Chilled through with the biting atmosphere of this dark world, and bewildered in its mazes, 'then I'll look up.' There the day-star shines to guide me home, and there the blessed Sun of Righteousness, to cheer and warm me with rays of love while here.

"February 19.—

> 'Be near me when the light is low,
> When the blood creeps and the nerves prick
> And tingle, and the heart is sick,
> And all the wheels of being slow.
> Be near me when the sensuous frame
> Is racked with pangs that conquer trust,
> And time a maniac scattering dust,
> And life a fury flinging flame,
> Be near me.'

"And why? Not to lighten the burden of grief when the mind is bowed down with its weight; not to soothe the aching brow or quivering nerves when the body is racked with pain, but to act as a sentinel upon the wandering fancies, and call back the wild vagaries of the unsettled mind. Poor human reason, distracted by the strange contradictions of this 'wondrous, weary, unintelligible world,' is not left to wander alone amid the night of years. Solitude is delightful to a contemplative mind, but to most natures its unrestrained indulgence is dangerous. Different minds, with their various errors, like the opposite influences of the planets in our system, in the end compensate each other. But a single one, unconnected, stretching out on the sea of thought, pursues the still vanishing solution of the great problems of life and death, God and man, being and dissolution, till out of sight of shore, befogged in the midst of ignorance, bewildered by the contradictory voices of nature and his own soul, and drifted away by the currents of passion and of pride, he becomes 'a wanderer o'er eternity, whose bark drives on and on, and ne'er shall anchored be.' Let the soul build realms for herself which shall never be realized, and people them with beings that shall never exist, but check the first budding of crude speculation, and forbid the first interrogation of impertinent inquiry.

"It is night. We should dwell upon beauties not found upon earth, and even grow familiar with dreams of happiness which this life shall never see.

"February 24.

'How glorious, how majestic is yonder setting sun,
'Tis thus the hero falls, 'tis thus he dies in godlike majesty.'

I was reading to-day of an interview between Bayard Taylor and the Baron Von Humboldt, at the close of which the veteran traveler took the hand of his younger rival and said: 'You have traveled much, and seen many ruins. You have now seen another.' To which Taylor responded: 'Not a ruin; a *pyramid!*' A pyramid indeed. The drifting sands of the desert shall sooner swallow up those of the Nile than the dust of ages bury the story of his wanderings. They may have served to conceal the treasures of kings; but his researches assisted to develope those of the King of kings. They may have answered as tombs for the Ptolemies, but he dragged to light secrets concealed since before the Ptolemies were. If such a man be not great, what is true greatness? Does it consist in the perfect training of Gustavus Adolphus, the schoolmaster of war, or in the reckless bravery of Charles XII., or in the eccentricity of Frederic William, and his brigade of seven-footers? These all acted their part in the drama of the world, and thousands of others have figured, and will figure, upon the same stage. But there is an arena grander still, where, instead of the boundaries of empire, the boundaries of thought are extended, and where the victims are not regiments of soldiers, but ignorance and prejudice. A soldier may be great. A conqueror may be a hero; he may stem the tide of despotism, and break the fetters of opposition. But he is not great in his calling, or even in his success. He is great only when his object is great. But he who spends his life in conquering the obstacles to human improvement, and in enlarging the range of human knowledge, and increasing the material for thought, is great in himself, in his calling, and in his success.

"February 18. There is to me something peculiarly pleasant in those creations of fancy which the soul conjures up as a kind of offset to the duller realities of life, as if to compensate herself for her uncongenial surroundings. Whilst clogged with the corporeal incumbrance, she takes advantage of moments of vacancy to wander off into an airy realm of her own, and to expatiate amid its ærial beauties. Becoming itself a portion of the world of its own creating, far from the gross contacts of real life, it finds its congenial residence where no jar disturbs the unbroken harmony, and no sorrow intrudes upon unmingled happiness. Now, instead of condemning these airy flights, they seem to me a beautiful evidence of something nobler in man than the present state is able to develope, something to which pollution is foreign, and discord painful, and which, in itself, looks to a future for deliverance from a painful captivity. Instead of chaining down the imagination to the narrow limits of daily routine, and circumscribing the mind to its range of observation, I would encourage it to rise higher and higher in its flight, and breathe an atmosphere purer and purer, as it leaves the rank effluvia that reeks up from the seething caldron of sordid selfishness, open debauchery, and secret crime, until bathing its broad wing with confident nativity in its proper element, it basks again in the undimmed radiance of heaven. There the shackles will drop off, and, above the world, angels will be its companions, and God its sun and shield.

"March 3. I have just received a letter from a dear friend, recording the goodness of God in taking him 'from the horrible pit and miry clay.' Bless the Lord, O my soul! But indeed his story is a sad one—all his fond hopes of love, and home, and happiness, suddenly swept away. No wonder his faith reeled under the blow. No wonder the heavens seemed like brass, and the earth like iron, long before he was softened, and so humbled as to say, 'Thy will be done.' May He who giveth songs in the night, still comfort and sustain him."

"March 7. * * * But after all, how fantastic are all my woes! How puerile my causes of despondency! It is true there are graves in my heart, both of hopes and friends. But I have life, and energy, and something burning within, turning my brain to fire, and my blood to lava, and my muscles to steel, as I almost shout to enter the battle-field, and try my strength with men upon the arena of life. I chafe like a caged eagle. I long to try my wings on the unmeasured expanse, and my secret soul never doubts of success. But when shall I obtain the power? Except a mass of thought, struggling for utterance, and finding none, and a will that compels all but impossibilities, I know I have but little. Yet, He who has led me hitherto, can use as humble an instrument as I for His glory. Do not say I am moved by pride of place. I think I am willing to labor wherever duty calls. For myself I care not. Labor, and toil, and penury; penury, labor, and toil, will doubtless mark the weary cycles of my pilgrimage upon earth, and I shall be content if I enjoy the smile of my Father in Heaven. But I am ambitious to stand in the front rank of those who turn many to righteousness. Lay the coal from thy altar upon my lips, O purifying Spirit, and breathe upon my cold heart, that it may glow with new life."

"April 8. The sky, so clear all day, has been suddenly overcast. The clouds are thick and dark, and the old trees are waving their arms wildly as an unchained maniac. If Virgil and a few others had not described storms, I should be tempted to do so! But the world is pretty well posted on that subject, so I forbear. It seemed to me, however, that Jupiter Tonans, grasping the lightning in his glittering right hand, and the more enlightened idea of 'our God, who plants his footsteps in the sea, and rides upon the storm,' is the irresistible impression of such a scene.

"That the peaceful, silent air, that sleeps in the shady valley—the balmy zephyr that kisses the invalid's cheek—'the sweet south wind that breathes upon a bank of violets,' should awake to such a fearful energy without the stimulus of an Omnipotent hand, seems incredible. And when the fierce coursers are unbound, who but God could lay his hand upon their manes, and bind them to His chariot?

"But who can feel the pressure of a present sublimity and then mould his thoughts to words? The mirror returns an image, dimmed, it is true, but faithful. The air transmits the thunder's sound with diminished power, but it is thunder still. Even in death we trace some feeble remains of its empire over clay; but neither mirror, nor medium, nor image, has the soul to shadow forth its unwritten volumes, or give expression to its soundless tones.

"April 9.—
>
> Across the valley Acheronian,
> Speak the dead in song and story;
> But the soul in depth Plutonean,
> Hides away its secrets hoary.
> The bard may reach the night Cimmerian,
> With not a ray upon its shore,
> When upward to the bright Hyperian
> With tireless, mounting, fancy soar;
> But pen and word, and thought and tongue,
> Have left the soul untold, unwritten, and unsung.

"Mrs. North says she invoked the harp of the north. But instead of that I got to the very opposite extreme. Well, perhaps the language is a little Tartarian, but I shall insist the only fault the idea has is, that it is too true to be poetic. Mrs. North sympathetically adds, that she never saw a poor wanderer so tempest tossed from the lowest depths up to Cimmerian, and then up to Hyperian. Well, it was a considerable distance to ride a muse in the space of ten lines. It must almost equal Mahommed's dromedary! Dear, kind woman! If the blessing of the stranger can in any degree lighten the human lot, surely yours will shine more and more unto the perfect day.

"April —. Busy all day: nothing done. And so life passes. How many vain regrets; how many fruitless resolutions; how many puerile efforts, make up the sum total of a man's history! Life is scarcely a strife. In the experience of most men, it is an unquiet lingering on the outskirts of the battle-field, without the resolution to enter the lists until the sun goes down. The herald proclaims the contest over, and the laurels are not won. The war, indeed, is in our ears all the day long. We see the success and failures of the combatants all around us. But we delay and dally; we 'resolve and re-resolve, and die the same.' Especially now, our flaccid muscles, and effeminated frames, are no longer fit tenements for the iron wills, and unconquerable resolution, of our ancestry. I am not disposed to depreciate the present race, and unduly exalt the more gross and unrefined state of society from which our forefathers emerged, but I do think that, as a nation and people, we are becoming *French*, in a geometrical ratio, and soon, lawless indolence, and aimless flippancy, will have supplanted the radical virtues of simplicity, economy, and energy.

"April 15. I have not sufficient elasticity, either of mind or feeling, to interest myself in the process of writing. What a strangely constituted being I am, or I might extend the range to include my fellow-worms, and say *we*. We swim in a sea of pleasure, and think 'life too fair for aught so fleeting,' and then, without a real cause, we writhe in agony, as if our bed were suddenly turned to lava. 'Now what is Hecuba to me, or me to Hecuba?' And yet I am sad almost beyond control. The current of life is flowing smoothly in my veins; my friends are kind as ever; my prospects as good as they were wont to be, and yet the folly of a silly boy or two can depress my spirit till my heart is almost ready to relieve itself in tears.

"Through the mists around me the phantom appears a monster, clothed with Gorgon horrors, and with all my resolution I cannot shake off the incubus that weighs upon me. But were my trials all that my fancy paints them, 'or worse than worst of those that lawless and uncertain thoughts imagine,' why should the spirit that claims affinity with the Deity, a link midway between two worlds, an interest to all the intelligent universe, for which angels labor, and devils howl, and God himself bled,— why should that which roams at will through the illimitable fields of knowledge, and the still grander field of imagination, be chafed and galled by the discomforts and difficulties of an inch of space, and a point of time? 'O, what a mystery is man to man! I wonder at myself and in myself am lost.'

—— "Time seems, for the last week or two, to pass slowly, while, before, it went with lightning speed. The approaching May, with its excitements, and the prospect of my own examination, makes the difference, I presume. The time of my sojourn here seems almost at a close. But a little more than three months, and the places that know me now, shall know me no more. My heart will be very sad at parting from the few friends who have strewed my path with all the happiness I have enjoyed, and whose like I may not hope to see again; who forgave faults none the less readily because they give acute and peculiar pain, and who seem, with all my faults, to love me still. O, what a world Heaven must be, where all the inhabitants are pure benevolents, and the God of love over all!

"April 16. Came home and found a most beautiful vase of flowers on my table; roses, and pinks, and camelias,—beautiful and rare! Blessings on the giver! Those lovely evidences of the goodness of God meet me like angel messengers, and point my groveling thoughts to heaven.

> 'Sweet fields beyond the swelling tide,
> Stand dressed in living green,'

and our heavenly Father shows His goodness in nothing more than strewing our pathway here with these lovely, silent, eloquent, messengers of a good God to His prodigal children.

"April 19. If we view life from the mere stand-point of time, it is indeed a failure. It is at best but a sad experiment. Sad, even when most successful. Even when our hoary heads are crowned with honor, we but go down to the grave, and mix with the commonest dust at last, and 'he died,' is the suming up of man's history. But few, as far as life is intrinsically considered, would endure life, and none would live it over again. 'What is all this worth?' is the natural inquiry of all men, after tasting all that life can afford. But when considered in the great light of eternity, it becomes a very different matter. When ten thousand ages have rolled away; when the lights that shone on creation's dawn, and which shall shine unchanged upon its night, shall have burnt out their fires, and fallen back into their original chaos; when all things shall be old but God, and the spirits which he breathed into existence; when the present shall have become the hoary past, and the past shall be forgotten,—then, in our separate individualities, we shall know the value of life. 'It is a tale told by an idiot,' for its meaning, its fearful meaning, is mistaken. It is but an unquiet wandering in a strange land, for our home lies beyond. 'Guide me, O Thou great Jehovah!' May this not only be a new year of my life, but a year of a new life. (Written on his birthday.)

"May 3. Chilly and damp—fit representation of this world of ours. It is true I have comfortable apartments, and a cheerful fire, by which I place my great arm-chair and enjoy the genial warmth; but clouds are over the face of the sky, and the great sun is obscured, while the rain patters unceasingly, or, driven by the cold wind, beats against my casement. So in life, we gather around us our little world, wrap ourselves in the comforts and enjoyments of our homes, and warm ourselves by the rays of human love, and while our roof-tree is firm, and our fire goes not out, we may close our eyes and ears for a little. But it is still true, notwithstanding, that, outside, all is cold, and dark, and our habitation is in the midst of dreariness and gloom, into which we may be driven by our falling structures, and feel ourselves to be, what we really are, orphan wan-

derers through 'a gloom, pierced by no star.'
The heathen poet said, two thousand years ago,
'We are also his offspring,' and the apostle of
the Gentiles endorsed the sentiment. But ah!
there lies the saddest element in our melancholy condition. If we had not been the
handiwork of God, and his subjects by creation, we could never bear about with us His
wrath. We would never feel working in us
that repellant power, born of rebellion, and
compounded of hatred and fear. Had not the
light of a Father's love shone upon the dawn
of our race, as the first happy pair came pure
from the hands of their Maker, we would never
have known the meaning, the fearful meaning,
of our present desolation. Conscious of guilt,
and pursued for ever by the voice of justice,
crying, 'Pay me that thou owest,' no wonder
we fly as far as possible from that purity and
holiness which we can never satisfy, and, by an
easy transition, from fearing we pass to hatred.
Truly we are worse than orphans; worse than
the spawn of the wandering beggar, for we are
the outcasts of a palace, miserable exiles from

a paradise; princes of a magnificent domain, sold into bondage; bright-eyed sons of the morning groping in blindness and agony through the cheerless night. Sun-kissed dwellers among vine-clad hills, we are surrounded with the bleak snows of an eternal winter. O, we are the fallen turrets of a magnificent structure, upon every stone of which is written, ruin, desolation, and decay! And worst of all, the sword hangs over us; not only to prevent our restoration, but it goes on hewing to pieces the fallen fragments, and pursuing them to the four winds! O, what a terrible sword it is! It never but once found an object on which it could full flesh its trenchant edge.

"May 23.—

> O! why should human love and hope
> But blossom into grief?
> Help, Father! In this maze I grope,
> And tears are my relief.
> But bleed my heart: I need the pain,
> To purge the dross away.
> So sorrows brighten future gain,
> As night adorns the day.

"There are but few things in the world that seem to me really proper subjects for sadness. There are times, it is true, when my feelings are depressed, and I cannot even persuade myself that I have a legitimate cause. But when my feelings are touched through the medium of my affections, I succumb at once. My sadness is all the more uncontrolable, because reflection but increases the intensity of the coloring. And unless I can persuade myself to repudiate the very feelings and characteristics which constitute my individuality, and become a mere link in the concatenation of things, which would fit as well in another place as in the one I occupy, I can find no palliative."

There are a number of notes which appear to be parts of his journal to which no dates are prefixed. Some of these will close the present chapter. Having referred to certain prevailing habits and associations, in Natchez, which were trials of faith, he adds: "I hope I shall be able to do my simple duty, and trust in God. But unless his spirit be present to aid me with his Divine power and guidance, I shall fail.

<blockquote>
'Guide me, O Thou great Jehovah,
Pilgrim through this barren land.'
</blockquote>

"Heard to-day of the acquittal of G——, on trial for swindling, or rather embezzling of funds to a large amount in New Orleans. Most probable his acquittal was owing to his guilt; so that 'the condition trammelled up the consequence,' and the man 'pardoned for parting with a part of the offence.' So the best security of life and property can be bought and sold. 'In the corrupted currents of this world, offence's gilded hand may shove by justice, and oft 'tis seen the wicked prize itself buys out the law. But 'tis not so above. *There* is no shuffling.'

—— "If Religion were a fable, what a fable it would be! How philosophical in doctrine! How far-sighted in precept! How philanthropic in spirit! How noble in object! How sublime in its consummation! That such a scheme should spring from nothing, is more incredible than that the great world, and all that is in it, should spring from nothing. If its origin was in the unsubstantial flights of a distempered fancy, then let us all turn dreamers, for no elaboration of thought, no deductions of reason, no painfully collated improvements upon the experience of all the past, ever have attained, or ever will approach, the simple sublimity, and profound and undeniable wisdom of its truths.

"The wisest among the heathen were bewildered and amazed with what they saw around them. But they dared not advance to the great solution with boldness, for it seemed a thing incredible that God should raise the dead. With the more humble, tradition solved the mystery, and all was clear. The intellectual Titans of the German school exhaust their energies in striving to brutify and degrade what the Bible has ennobled and dignified. The widow in her cottage is content to believe; man is honored, and God is glorified. Truly, the foolishness of God is wiser than men, and the weakness of God is stronger than men.

—— "I think I must be about to experience

some great good, 'for we all know that security is mortal's chiefest enemy.' To me there is such a sense of uneasiness, that 'over all there hangs the shadow of a fear. A sense of mystery has the spirit daunted,' and says in every breath, and every word, 'sorrow awaits thee.' But poor Ephemeron, why swells your heart with pain, or why does it leap with joy, when the poor rag upon which your thoughts are inscribed may far outlive your earthly joys and sorrows. Strange comment upon human fame, when it depends for perpetuation upon material so feeble and transient! So in a sense, the sacred poet did not anticipate. Man is crushed before the moth. When a hundred years have rolled away, where shall I be, and where shall be my memory? In the mighty past it will glimmer faintly, or perhaps it may have ceased even to glimmer. And yet my appetite for immortality is insatiable. 'It must be. Cato, thou reasonest well.' And after all, what a melancholy thing is human greatness, purchased, as it must be, either by the corrosion of one's own spirit, by the energy of internal fire that burns, and burns, until the poor wretch is consumed by his own vitality, or by the groans of other victims, sacrified on the altar of his ambition. 'There is no release in that war.' There is no greatness without suffering. From the grave of a suicide, Hugh Miller speaks, O, so eloquently! of the madness of it all. The untiring energy and dauntless perseverance that grappled with every difficulty, and manfully wound his way up to the summit of his ambition, then grew dizzy and reeled; half recovered,—the deadly weapon is in his hand; a spasm, and all is over. How are the mighty fallen!"

Writing, in the early spring, of birds, and flowers, and fruits, of fig and orange blossoms, he says: "Such things as these tell me that I am a wanderer. But I read it everywhere, from my own heart to the very stars I gazed upon under a more inhospitable sky. Even the heavens here are strange. The Great Bear hides himself during part of the night below the horizon, while the ship of Argos comes up in the south, and stares at me with its great eyes, as if to tell me that I am a stranger.

"Last Sabbath, Rev. Dr. Stratton took the position, that ambition is the most powerful passion in the human breast. It may be so; and there are reasons why our intellectual and immortal being should be more likely to yield to the influence of ambition than to any other passion. But the objects of ambition are as various as its empire is large. From Bolingbroke's gross desire to be preëminent in dissipation and sensuality, to the sacred ambition of excelling in goodness, there is every shade and degree. But, after all, it is selfishness, and very short-sighted at that. How like apples of Sodom are its rewards and its crowns. 'What are ye now but thorns about my bleeding brow,' is the feeling of its most successful devotees.

   'Small have continual plodders ever won
     Save base authority from others books.—*Shakspeare.*

   'Much study is a weariness of the flesh.—*Bible.*

Now, I do not repudiate all study. I think a 'soul without reflection, like a pile without inhabitant, to ruin runs.' But why should we waste our hours in loading our memories with the fancies of other men, while mines of unelaborated thought lie neglected in our own souls? Simply for one reason. It is easier to read than to think; to remember than to reflect; to appropriate than to originate. Our literary pampering has done for our minds what our more luxuriant mode of life is doing for our bodies: refined, and made more elegant perhaps; but where are the giant frames, and iron muscles of our hardy sires? We read the lofty soarings of Milton, and the infinite variations of the versatile Shakspeare, the wonderful inductions of Bacon, and the far-reaching analysis of Newton, but instead of rousing ourselves to emulate their fame, we say, truly, 'there were giants in those days.' We are growing refined and sentimental, or skeptical and metaphysical; and instead of elaborating the important problems of ethics and physics, which are yet unsolved, we take to 'splitting hairs 'twixt south and south-west side,' and think we are profound because we are unintelligible. But, I suppose if I were in the olden time, forecasting the future, I would pine for the refinement and books of the nineteenth century.

—— "Heard Dr. Palmer on the text: 'How is my soul troubled.' If his bodily presence is weak, his speech is by no means contemptible. Although his declamatory power is by no means so high as estimated by some, he has a great deal of nervous physical power, and his style of thought is strong and remarkably clear, so that the whole discourse seems impressed on the mind as a unity, over which you can look, and recall almost every idea. After introducing his subject by a description of the sorrows to which man is heir in life, from the cradle to the grave, he remarked, that the Man of Sorrows was pre-ëminently experienced in them all. He then went on to enumerate the different elements in His sufferings at the time he gave utterance to the words of the text. They were: First, An overwhelming sense of His responsibilities. Second, Instinctive and human horror at the sense of approaching death. Third, The contact, and burden of sin that was laid upon Him—all viewed as an indication of the love of God, and as a vindication of the sovereignty of His attributes."

Speaking of the excitement of election days in Natchez, he writes: "I looked at the banners streaming—the fire blazing—the torches sparkling—the fire-balls, red, white, and blue, exploding hundreds of feet high in the air—the balloons ascending and floating away to the north—the motley crowd, black, brown, and white, swaying under the influence of intense excitement around the speaker's stand, till wearied, and sick at heart, with all the glitter and glare of false patriotism, and real duplicity, I withdrew from the crowd, and wended my way home.

"It is a glorious night. Old Orion, the Pleiades, and Hyades, Procyon, and Capella, look down like holy things on a sinful world; so calm, so beautiful. I thought of the glory and beauty of God's House. I thought too of the dear friends who had watched the same stars with me under a more inclement sky. O, my quiet home! To-day we heard of the Lamb of God, who taketh away the sin of the world; to-morrow we commemorate His death. Strange medley! At these times my thoughts revert, O, how tenderly! to the home of my childhood, and I feel strengthened by the assurance, that for me prayers continually ascend, in the earnestness of true devotion, to the ears of the Lord of Sabaoth."

Now he takes his last survey of the natural beauties which he is about to leave, and then remarks: "If it were not for sin, what a beautiful world this would be, and what a beautiful thing life would be! But *that* poisons every cup, and embitters every joy. Suspicion and treachery, mistrust and deceit, grow alike on that fatal tree. O, God, when will the curse have an end!"

From the pleasant scenes and associations of the sunny south, he turned away, never to return, his thoughts elevated to that world where the broken chain of human affection will be reunited, and the sad word "farewell" will never be spoken.

CHAPTER VI.

STUDENT IN THE THEOLOGICAL SEMINARY.

Soon after leaving Natchez, Mr. Thom entered the Theological Seminary at Princeton, New Jersey. He conscientiously conformed to all the rules of that institution, was a diligent student, and gathered knowledge from every available source. His range of theological reading was wide, and with several Latin authors he became so familiar, that he could quote from them with remarkable accuracy. Turretine's works were thoroughly mastered, and he considered himself more indebted to these for what theological attainments he had made, than to any other human production. He placed a high estimate upon the advantages enjoyed in the Seminary, and was ever after an enthusiastic friend of that honored "school of the prophets."

Not by study only, but by the cultivation of personal piety, also, he sought preparation for the great work before him. He observed seasons of fasting and prayer, and derived much benefit from religious conversation with a few intimate friends. To him the "Conference Meetings" were very profitable, and very precious. In his letters he made frequent reference to these. He learned much of Jesus and much of himself in those "family gatherings;" the professors addressing the students with the tenderness of parental love, dwelling in simple, earnest utterances on the great themes of Christian experience, the fulness of Christ, and duty to the Master.

Very little occurs in a student's life to disturb the "even tenor of his way," and Mr. Thom adhered so closely to the routine of Seminary duty, that to record the labors of a week, would be to present a miniature photograph of his entire course. The remainder of the chapter will be chiefly occupied with letters, which reveal the fervor of his piety, and his healthful growth in the Divine life.

On a day set apart for fasting and prayer, he writes to a friend: "I am endeavoring to approach the throne of grace in my own behalf to-day, that God would fit me for the work of the ministry. I wish you could unite in concert with me; but it is now too late for that. O, I need, so much, more grace, and devotion, and love! I know, my friend, that you pray for me, but I am afraid that, well as you know me, you think me much better than I am, and so cannot really adapt your prayers to my case. I am very sinful. God only knows, and He only can remedy, my wickedness. O, pray continually all these weeks, and months, and years, that I may be more and more furnished for every good work. I am every day more and more impressed with the feeling that mere human strength can never avail me anything. 'All my strength must come from God.' ... It is a reflection of no ordinary solemnity, that I sit daily in the halls where Alexander and Miller taught, and live in the rooms whose walls have been hallowed by the prayers of Walter

Lowrie and kindred spirits, who have gone to their reward. O! that the same Spirit which breathed upon them, might be infused into me, making me a 'temple of God.' ... I have just returned from prayer-meeting, a precious and solemn meeting."

A college acquaintance had entered the ministry before him, and was laboring with much success in one of the western States. Intelligence was received, by a fellow-student, of a precious work of grace in progress in the young pastor's charge. With Mr. Thom it was a time of thanksgiving. "Blessed be His holy name." He thus writes to a dear friend: "You of course have heard of the revival at M——. A friend here has just received a letter from Mr. B——, giving an account of it. On coming to the church on Sabbath, he could scarcely enter, because of the crowd at the door. When he had gained admittance to the church, he found the aisles, pulpit-stairs, and even the pulpit, full of people, and a most powerful work seemed going on—some fifty, at that date, inquiring the way to Zion. O, what a day seems dawning! In our prayer-meeting for Colleges, this morning, three were reported as being greatly blessed. Every paper brings good tidings, and our hearts seem to be responding. I felt a good deal encouraged this morning, and then at noon, when I heard of the revival at M—— my heart was melted.... Let us, though separated, daily pray that God's kingdom may come. Pray for *me*, that in due time utterance may be given me to preach the infinite love of God. I feel, more and more, that all my sufficiency is of God, as all the glory must be His.

"Monday morning. We had a most interesting conference yesterday, on the constraining love of Christ. I wish I could tell it all to you. But I hope you know better from your own heart than any one could tell you, what the love of Christ is. It passeth knowledge."

Soon after, he was rejoiced to hear of a precious revival at Canonsburg. The students in the Seminary, who were graduates of Jefferson College, met every Sabbath morning to pray for the outpouring of the Holy Spirit on that institution. Some time in March, 1857, Mr. Thom received cheering news from his Alma Mater, and rising in the night, he wrote in thankful strains concerning the Lord's doing, which was marvellous in his eyes. "It is half past 3 o'clock, A. M., but I cannot sleep with your letter before me. What glad tidings of great joy it contains! My poor, weak faith, was not prepared for such intelligence. Your previous letter contained an account of the communion services, and no unusual interest then. This is a critical and most interesting time. O, for a spirit of prayer! O, for a revival of God's work in our own hearts, and such a revival that we shall never grow cold again! How I wish we could meet and mingle our prayers, for God does often make use of human sympathy to warm the fire of sacred, divine love. My only hope is, that He who was touched with a feeling of our infirmities will pity my weakness. God be merciful to us, and bless us, and cause His face to shine upon us. I trust my heart is a little revived, but my coldness is more apparent than before. Like one coming from the cold air to a heated atmosphere, I am becoming sensible that I was much chilled. O, pray much for me..... I have been to Trenton, to hear Everett. At another time I would have had much to tell you. Now I am thinking of something greater than Everett, and better than Washington."

To one who "walked in darkness, and saw no light," he addressed wise counsel in a letter from which the following extract is taken: "You know, dear friend, as well as I do, the sources of spiritual happiness. But, may it not be, we both sometimes forget what God has done for us? It is true there is much, very much, yet to be done. But if he has done that which is greatest, shall we not thank God, and take courage? Instead of repining because all our sins are not overcome, let us adore that love that spared not the Son of God, and when we are cast down, let us look at ourselves only enough to feel we need a Saviour, and then *fly to Him*...... There is one thing more which I know tends to keep me away from Christ, and perhaps more than anything else; that is, resting on the fact that He died for *sinners*, without clearly feeling that He died for *me*. And yet that is the very essence of faith. O, if we could see Jesus offering Himself for us, surely our faith would work by love."

Writing to another, he says: "The great subject now is the grand celebration in New York, in honor of the laying of the Atlantic Cable, the largest meeting ever held, I suppose, on the American continent, and a larger one than would be allowed on the greater part of the old one. The only way I have heard the people estimated, is by the acre, and miles. Broadway, for nearly, or quite four miles, was one almost impenetrable mass, the crowd swaying back and forth, hour after hour. O, if the cable is worth so much, *what should be done for one soul!* ..... Had a long letter from L. C., who thinks my greatest temptation is to pride. Perhaps it is. God forbid that I should glory in anything save in the cross of our Lord Jesus Christ, and through it may the word be crucified to me, and I unto the world."

Whilst at Princeton, Mr. Thom made direct efforts for the conversion of sinners around him. He taught in a Sabbath-school, and occasionally conducted a service for the colored people. He also visited neglected places in the vicinity of Princeton, and sought opportunities of addressing perishing souls on the subject of personal religion.

Speaking to one, of his earnest desire to have his armor on, and all his energies directly given to the work of the ministry, he said, "It is a consummation I devoutly wish, and yet I shrink back from it. I can scarcely analyze my feelings. But I feel it is a dreadful thing to stand between the living and the dead. If it be shrinking from duty, may God forgive me: if a true sense of my unworthiness, may He grant me more grace and faith."

At another time, writing to a friend, he regretfully refers to causes which had kept him back from his profession. He could scarcely keep from repining at a destiny which had robbed him of his youth, and burdened his manhood with an almost crushing load of care. But he endeavored to calm his mind by the reflection that God does all things well, and that all his trials would be blessed to his greater fitness for the ministry. And it is no doubt a fact, that those four years of labor as a teacher, were not only years of usefulness, but did go far to develope those traits of character which made him eminent as a pastor, and successful as a preacher.

Whilst engaged in teaching, he anticipated some of the studies of the theological course, and remained in the Seminary only two years. During the holiday-vacation of the second session, in January, 1859, he was licensed to preach the gospel by the Presbytery of Saltsburg, at Leechburg, Pennsylvania. His extraordinary endowments of every kind for ministerial efficiency, and his remarkable pulpit power, early developed, and so highly matured, were not matters of surprise to the members of Presbytery who had known him intimately for years. All predicted for the young licentiate a ministry of great usefulness. After licensure he returned to the Seminary, and devoted himself with increased earnestness to study, during the remainder of the session. To a friend, who urged him to take a season of recreation, fearing the results of the close application to Seminary duties, he said, "I look for no rest this side of the grave." Before the close of the session he received several calls to vacant churches. One, to a southern state, presented special inducements in the way of worldly comfort, but he felt constrained to decline it, feeling that there were other fields of labor where he was more needed, and might be more useful. He was also invited to take a prominent charge in the west, and this he felt strongly inclined to accept. At one time he had seriously considered the question of going to a foreign field, but he presently found insuperable barriers in the way, and yielded to the force of what were then very sad and trying providences. And now that he must labor in some part of his own country, he preferred a missionary field in the west. He would plant the standard of the cross on the borders of the wilderness, and aid the worn and weary men who toiled for Jesus in regions "near the sunset."

Then came an urgent call from the church at Waynesburg, Pennsylvania. At first he entertained scarcely a thought of accepting it. Not that he was unwilling to cross the deep yearnings of his heart to go to a far different field, but he was not satisfied that the Head of the Church would have him occupy a position which so many others were willing to fill, whilst there were destitutions where the call for ministerial labor seemed so much louder. He submitted the matter to the Lord, and waited further revelations of the Master's will. At length the indications of Providence pointed clearly to Waynesburg. All anxious questionings as to duty were answered, and before he left the Seminary he announced his acceptance of the call, so unexpectedly and earnestly pressed upon him. "The steps of a good man are ordered by the Lord: and he delighteth in his way."

In this connection we introduce a letter, written by Rev. Robert Strong, of Albany, N. Y., an intimate friend of our deceased brother. Mr. Strong was, for a short time, pastor of the Westminster Presbyterian Church in Minneapolis, Minnesota. This statement will explain the latter part of his letter.

"Mr. Thom entered the Seminary at Princeton at the same time I entered, in 1857. I was early attracted to him by his friendliness and kindliness, and as our acquaintance deepened with familiar intercourse, I prized his friendship more and more. He was one of the substantial men of the class, above the average in abilities, and far above in mature disciplined Christian character. After he had graduated at College, (Jefferson, I think,) he spent several years in teaching, not with a view of delaying his entrance into the ministry, nor as a partial preparation to it, but with the sole view, as I understood him, of enabling him to pass through the Seminary independently, unaided either by loans or by grants from the Board of Education. He could not submit himself to dependence or to charity. We had many a friendly debate together as to whether such a course is generally right, and whether men who have given themselves wholly to the Church of God, ought not to thankfully receive every aid that will hasten the period of active usefulness, or enlarge it. If he made a mistake here, it was the mistake of a strong character; not underrating the loving provision of the Church, but despising a mean or unnecessary dependence upon it. I do not think it was a pride to be condemned, for it partook of the spirit which led St. Paul to labor with his own hands, 'that he might not be chargeable to any,' though at the same time counting himself a 'servant for Jesus' sake.'

"Having this spirit, the years spent in teaching did not in the least lessen his earnest look toward the ministry. He made them as truly years of preparation as if they had been spent in the Seminary, pursuing the same studies and courses of reading, and looking as directly to the end. The result was, that he entered the Seminary in 1857, with his earnestness and resolution tested by the delay he had enforced on himself, able to sustain himself unaided, with superior preparation, direct purpose, and a character trained and strong.

"I do not think Mr. Thom was fully appreciated in the Seminary. His standard was too high for many, his honest nature revolted at anything like meanness or false shame, and he was often pained by low estimates of the sacred ministry, and of full consecration to Christ. He was not solitary, nor in the least censorious, but, on the contrary, kind, sympathetic, and genial, in a marked degree, yet he walked and thought above the mass. Those only could appreciate him whom he specially liked, and to whom he would unfold himself. I spent many evenings with him in his room, in long conversations and reading, and it was there I found him out, manly, strong-hearted, proud to a fault, warm-hearted, gentle as a woman, with a mind well stored and well trained, earnest in devotion, and a real lover of the Saviour. I saw then that he had great capabilities as a preacher, a ready utterance, power and warmth. In his Seminary exercises he evidently repressed his warmth, as if unduly careful to be right in what he said. But the glow of a warm heart was not to be concealed, and it must have been the source of his power afterwards.

"After we both left the Seminary, our correspondence was interrupted by mutual cares. I much regret now that, on account of frequent removals, my letters of those days have been all destroyed. The last time I heard from him was in 1863, in response to an invitation to take charge of, and oversee, our mission work in Minnesota, as Synodical Missionary. He replied, that he would like to come west, and that he thought such a position would meet all his desires, but that the circumstances of his church at Waynesburg would not permit his leaving at that time. He promised, however, to take it into more mature and prayerful consideration. We were much disappointed when he wrote again, that, though his desires were with us, the way was not clear. Had he been able to come, he would have left his mark on the state and on all our churches.

"His sudden death, after his removal to St.

Louis, was a great loss to our Church in the west, greater even than it was generally counted. Only those that knew him best, could appreciate the work he was fitted to do. We can only console ourselves with the old comfort, old but never worn, that God loves the Church and souls better than we do, and His servants and children can trust Him."

CHAPTER VII.

LABORS AT WAYNESBURG, PENNSYLVANIA.

LEAVING the Seminary, he went at once to the field of labor to which he had been called, and at a meeting of the Donegal Presbytery, held at Waynesburg, May 19, 1859, he was received, ordained, and installed pastor of the Waynesburg Church. That was to him a day of solemn interest; a day of thanksgiving to Christ Jesus our Lord, who had enabled him, for that he counted him faithful, putting him into the ministry. At the same time he was oppressed with a sense of fearful responsibility. Who is sufficient for these things? Surely, he said, "Except the Lord build the house, they labor in vain that build it. Except the Lord keep the city, the watchman waketh but in vain." What shall be the results of the relation just formed? How many souls shall be saved through his agency? or lost through his unfaithfulness? He invokes a fresh baptism of the Holy Spirit, puts on his armor, and trusting in Jesus only, he goes forth to the work of faith and labor of love.

He first took a survey of the field he was to cultivate, and endeavored to make himself acquainted with the spiritual condition of the church, that he might adapt himself to the necessities of the people, and wisely mature his plans of operation. The congregation extended over a territory of ten square miles. Pastoral visiting claims attention. The labor will be great and exhausting, but the necessity is absolute, and he entered upon it. One of his people wrote, "Our minister has a will and resolution which yield to nothing short of impossibilities."

He soon came to know all the families of his widely extended charge; could call nearly every child by name, and learned something of the religious history of the majority of his people. "Well do I remember," wrote a good woman, "his first visit to my home. His great care seemed to be for our spiritual interests. I had two little children: he took each of them by the hand, and told them of Jesus, who said, 'Suffer little children to come unto me.' He then led us all to the mercyseat, and commended us to the care of our covenant-keeping God. How it bound us to him! The burden of his prayers always was for the salvation of souls, and his solemn, earnest manner, could scarcely fail to impress the heart of an unconverted person."

It was not a matter of surprise that strong bonds of sympathy and affection soon united the pastor and his flock. He early wrote of his love to his church, and was thankful for evidences of healthful piety in many households. "They are so kind and considerate, and above all, they seem to have the spirit of prayer, and consecration to Jesus." But in some households there was no recognition of God in family prayer, and some who had run well had been hindered. There was not a little to distress, if not to discourage, the ardent pastor. But it was a time for work; faithful, earnest, affectionate work,—and he set about it. The spiritual diagnosis suggested the remedies. He soon established four weekly prayer-meetings in different parts of the congregation, attending them alternately two evenings of each week, and secured elders, or other members of the church, to conduct the services on the evenings of his absence. In addition to these, he had the regular prayer-meeting in the church, which was attended by the families residing in, and near the village. At the several points in the country, to which we have referred, he also held afternoon services on the Sabbath, and thus he carried the gospel to many families who had previously lived without it. He also taught a Bible-class, which met in the church before the Sabbath morning service. He devoted much time to his preparations, and the instruction imparted on these occasions were blessed to not a few. He was a patient teacher, and condescended to the capacities of the humblest; going over the oft repeated lesson, sweetly pressing Jesus on the acceptance of the young, and solemnly warning them of the consequences of unbelief. He was wont to say: "The word of God will not return unto Him void, and He who gave you this glorious gospel will be glorified, whether you reject or receive His gracious message."

The Sabbath-schools were frequently visited, and he usually addressed the children in loving, earnest words. A number of family altars were erected through his efforts. He assisted some of the young married members, by going to their houses soon after they entered them, and kindling the fire upon their altar, urging them, "so affectionately and earnestly," never to let that fire go out. It grieved him to learn that in some cases his efforts in behalf of family religion were attended with but very little fruit.

Parental responsibility was pressed home with great solemnity. One said, "I used to feel under his preaching that it was a fearful thing to be a parent." To a burdened mother, who had been much affected by his teachings on the subject of the religious training of children, he said: "To feel our own insufficiency for these things, brings us close to the cross, and surely if you can trust Jesus with your own salvation, you can trust him with the salvation of the children He has given you. Do your duty, and remind God of His covenant."

The first months of his ministry were marked by a special reviving in the church. He lifted the standard of piety high, dealt faithfully with those who lived in neglect of Christian duties, and were sadly conformed to the world. One who heard him preach for the first time, probably six months after his settlement, thought there was too much severity in his preaching, and ventured to suggest a change, at the same time referring to the wonderful power of Dr. P——, who was accustomed to give much prominence to the gentleness of Jesus, and the sweet attractions of the cross. Mr. Thom replied, that he had discovered many in his church who were wrapped in a mantle of self-satisfaction, and their estimate of themselves, he said, must be corrected. They answered to the description given of the Laodicean church, and it was not the time to preach pleasant things, however much he and others might enjoy the presentation of the precious things of God. The sequel proved that he was right. There was much searching of heart, conviction of worldliness, repentance of sin, and some turned unto the Lord, who had been content with a mere name to live. "We had got to think," said one, who had long been a member of the church, "that it was an easy thing to get to heaven." They had lost sight of the Saviour's declaration: "If any man will be my disciple, let him deny himself, and take up his cross, and follow me." Now they begin to realize that without cross-bearing, there can be no crown-wearing. Said a good elder, "Mr. Thom's people cannot listen long to his preaching without being able to determine whether they are Christians or not." And *then* many were heard asking, with much anxiety of mind,

"Do I love the Lord or no,
Am I His, or am I not?"

Soon after, there were indications of great seriousness among non-professors. The meetings for preaching and prayer were multiplied, and protracted as long as the interest seemed to warrant. At this time a considerable number expressed hope in Christ. The communion service was delayed for a season that these persons might have time for self-examination, and about forty-five persons were added unto the church, of such, we trust, as shall be saved. Some of these were heads of families. Parents came with their children, and were baptized together. Young men consecrated themselves to Christ, and proved valuable accessions to the church. Thus God early set the seal of his approbation upon the pastor's labors, and new ties were formed, binding preacher and people in Christian love and effort,—ties which grew continually stronger.

A few cases of interest in connection with this revival may be mentioned: There was one who attended the services in the church, and seemed to be under religious impressions;

a quiet, useful citizen, subdued by affliction, and respected by all. The sympathies of the pastor were drawn toward this man, and he sought opportunities of manifesting his interest in his spiritual welfare. One week-day, on his way to the church, Mr. Thom overtook this man, who was carrying several packages. He proposed to relieve him of a part of his load. The man thanked him for his kind offer, and added, that he needed help to bear far heavier burdens than those in his hands. Then, after a very sad conversation, he handed the minister a letter, which, he said, he had prepared for him. Mr. Thom took it home, and wept and prayed over it. Never, perhaps, was his soul so stirred within him as then, and for days together the sad wail which was the burden of the letter was sounding in his ears: "No man careth for my soul." That man had lived out more than half the period allotted to human life. He had associated with professing Christians for many years, had attended frequently, if not regularly, upon the public services of the church, and yet had never been addressed on the subject of personal religion. Such cases are doubtless exceptional, and there may have been something peculiar in this man's history, but this instance of unfaithfulness on the part of God's people was startling and humiliating. "Let him that heareth say, Come."

A lady of intelligence, high social position, and much influence in the community, was brought to feel her need of Christ. She was urged to believe in the Lord Jesus at once. She did not disguise the exercises of her mind, which disclosed a most critical condition. Her pastor was deeply concerned and anxious. At length she yielded to King Jesus, and her consecration was entire. Henceforth her home, like that of the holy family in Bethany, was ever open to the visits of the Heavenly Friend, and His sweet words, "Peace be to this house," brought with them light and gladness all unknown before.

Another was a member of the church: perhaps she had never been born again. During this season of religious interest she was awakened to a sense of danger. Her sins pressed heavily upon her. She walked in darkness, and saw no light. Her distress increased, day by day. Mr. Thom was instinctively drawn to her, learned her condition, and then pointed out the way of life so plainly, presented the sweet promises of the gospel so clearly, that the burdened soul saw the cross, hastened to it, and laid all her sins on Jesus, the spotless Lamb of God.

These may be taken as representative cases. There are volumes of unwritten history, which, if opened to the view of the church, would reveal the untiring vigilance, the patient toil, the tender faithfulness of the pastor. The judgment-day alone will disclose it fully.

At that time the church in Waynesburg was like Gideon's fleece, bedewed with the gently distilling grace of God, when, all around, the earth was dry; or like an oasis in the desert, watered and verdant, whilst silent barren sands stretched out on every hand. Again there were seasons when other churches were more abundantly refreshed, and the sovereignty of God was manifested. "Even so, Father, for so it seemeth good in thy sight."

In his first anniversary sermon he makes a grateful record of the Lord's doing among the people. Allusion was made to the labors of his predecessor,* who was greatly beloved by all the people, the fruits of whose labors were being gathered, and the people were called upon to praise the Lord, who had visited them with His salvation, and made the place of His feet glorious.

This year he had made nearly four hundred visits for conversation and prayer, beside many visits to the sick and dying. He had preached and lectured over four hundred times, and had spent much time with inquirers, and yet lamented that he had not been able to labor more.

During that year of refreshing, death had been very busy in the church. The message, "Prepare to meet thy God," came from nearly a score of new made graves, and some of the flock had gone to the greener pastures of the

* Rev. William W. Latta.

Better Land. "Sweet friends!" said the pastor, "we hope to meet them in heaven." Then were suggested some thoughts concerning the sorrows of this changeful life, and the eternal quiet of the skies. "As I occupy the place of him who is gone, so another shall soon stand in mine. I shall be forgotten, and all the generations to come shall remember me no more. We all must go to the land of silence and forgetfulness, and others shall worship in our room. But in the church above, there shall be no sundering of holy, happy ties. When we enter the temple on high, we shall be pillars in the temple of our God, and go no more out." Little, perhaps, did he or they suppose, on that first anniversary day, that so soon the pastor would be taken, that pulpit occupied by another, and these, his spiritual children, lamenting, "Alas, my father!"

In a later anniversary sermon, he referred with gratitude to the results of Christian labor, to the efforts of Sabbath-school teachers, especially of the female teachers, to induce neglected children to attend the Sabbath-school; to the faithfulness of different members, young men and others, who sustained prayer-meetings, and secured the attendance of the careless; to the Christian bravery with which many had taken up arms for Christ, in public and in private; to the consecration of worldly substance to Him who says of the gold and silver, "It is mine;" and to the Christian meekness with which the people had received the rebukes and admonitions of their pastor, administered in love, and for their good. "For all these things," said he, "I am glad, and I thank God for you always, making mention of you continually in my prayers." .

It was in the early part of his first year at Waynesburg, that one of the elders of the church (J. B.) was called to his eternal rest. He was constant in his attentions to the dying man, who was much of the time in great darkness, induced, doubtless, by physical causes. Mr. B—— was a good man, full of the Holy Ghost, and of faith. His life had exhibited the power of Divine grace, and the beauties of holiness, so clearly, that none who knew him questioned his meetness for heaven. It was not long until God brought him out of the darkness, and glory beamed upon the dying saint. One day, the light of heaven resting on his face, he said to his pastor, as he entered the death-chamber, "Have you come to rejoice with me, because I have found Him whom my soul loveth?" The latter sat down and wept. Those were tears of mingled joy and sorrow: of joy, that in the experience of the beloved elder the faithfulness of God was manifested, since at evening time it was light: of sorrow, that one so endeared to him by his beautiful Christian character, and so fitted to counsel and encourage the young pastor, was about to be taken. The following record refers to the deceased elder. "I am much exhausted with fatigue and excitement. For the last few days I have been seeing glory begun below. Bless the Lord, O my soul! And yet I weep, for I shall see his face no more."

About this time, June 9, 1857, the young minister was married to Miss Jennie M.

Bracken, of Canonsburg, Pennsylvania. They were both cordially received into the family of Mr. W. B——, a brother of the deceased elder. The generous hospitality of that home, enjoyed for a year, was never forgotten. No chill, like untimely September frosts, ever fell upon the pastor's affection for that loved and loving household. It was a pleasant reflection to him, that Christian kindness shall be rewarded here, and in the life to come. "Inasmuch as ye have done it unto one of the least of these, my brethren, ye have done it unto me."

Mr. Thom was very attentive to the bereaved. He told his people that when they were well and exempt from trials, they must allow him to pass by their homes, that he might devote more of his time to God's sorrowing ones. There are many who remember his kind and encouraging words, addressed to them in affliction. By not a few, they will doubtless be heard in years to come, reaching them across the intervening time, and lightening their burdened hearts, long after the tongue which uttered them was silenced in death. To a mother, whom he met at the door of her darkened home, he said, "God loved Mary, and He has taken her to Himself. There is comfort in this. Then remember that you have Christ still.

> 'He never takes away our all,
> Himself He gives us still.'"

Then they went together to Jesus and told Him all. The Lord comforted the bereaved parent, and enabled her to say, "Thy will be done." Very many similar instances might be mentioned, for there were but few families that were not called to endure like affliction.

The poor were specially bound to him. He not only sympathized with them; he contributed to their necessities. He often gave the last dollar to some needy sufferer. One who rode with him along a by-way, overheard some children of poverty, who, ashamed of their rags, endeavored to conceal themselves, say, "there is the good man who gave us money." He often urged kind and prompt attentions to such, and believed no church would be blessed which had none of God's poor in its communion. He induced a number of people who lived in humble homes, to come to the house of God. Through his word some believed in Christ, and are to-day journeying toward everlasting habitations, or have already entered them. "Blessed is he that considereth the poor. The Lord will deliver him in time of trouble." Psalm xli. 1. (Read James ii. 1—5, and Prov. xxii. 2.)

He did not confine his attentions to his own people. He visited, when necessary, the poor and afflicted of other churches; watching with the sick, carrying some delicacy to tempt the appetite, and by affectionate counsel, joined to expressions of sympathy, he lifted the burden from aching hearts.

Then, too, he was often called from home to aid his brethren in the ministry. He preached at many protracted meetings in different parts of the country, and never failed to meet an engagement, no matter what of self-denial it might cost. Then, when his work was done, he hastened home, to resume, with increased fidelity and earnestness, his labors among his own people.

He insisted much on attention to strangers. Though he had no sympathy with that selfishness which would make everything subservient to one's particular church, regardless of the claims of others, yet he would have attention shown to the visitor and traveler, and a cordial welcome extended to unknown persons who came to his church. A young man, who worshipped in another church, complained to him of the want he there felt of sympathy with the stranger. "It seemed to me," he said, "as if everybody had chartered his own private conveyance to heaven, and looked out at me over the closed door, as if to say, 'if you want to go, provide a conveyance for yourself.'" One reason why the large church in Waynesburg was filled on almost all occasions of public worship, was because of the courteous, Christian attention to the "stranger within their gates." Many who passed that way felt that it would be well if all our churches would emulate so worthy an example.

He felt, and manifested, a deep interest in young men. Several are now in the ministry, or in course of preparation for it, who were brought to Christ through his agency, and directed by him to that high and holy vocation. Poor young men, who struggled upward to higher and broader fields of usefulness, had his warm and loving sympathy. He sought them out in their discouragements, and resorted to many expedients to inspire them with faith and hope. Men of promise, one of whom is now gone to a far-off mission field,* have said: "For what we are, and all we hope to be, we owe more to Mr. Thom, so far as human agency is concerned, than to any man living, and no one ever exerted upon us so great an influence for good as he." His memory is precious to them, and through their word, he, being dead, yet speaketh.

His tact for adapting himself to all people and circumstances was very remarkable. The

* Rev. E. M. Wherry.

humblest and the lowliest had his tenderest thoughts, and they carried their troubles to him with childlike confidence, sure of sympathy, words of encouragement, and a helping hand. At the same time he secured the esteem of ministerial brethren, who were many years his seniors, and occupied positions of the highest influence in the church, and his general intelligence enabled him to commune with almost every class of literary and professional men. His versatility of talent was often remarked by men of learning and discernment, and was exceeded by few of his age.

He sought opportunities of conversing with the unconverted on the subject of personal religion, and sowed beside all waters. He made it a rule never to leave a fellow-traveler, or one with whom he held an hour's conversation at a hotel or watering-place, without dropping at least a word for Christ. Only eternity will reveal the results of such efforts to benefit souls. When riding over the many miles embraced in his parish, or going to preach in some neighboring church, he would ask the traveler along the dusty way-side to take a seat beside him in his carriage, and if he discovered that the stranger was without God and hope in the world, he would tell him of the way which led from the city of destruction to the Celestial City, and urge him to enter it at once.

Sometimes his anxiety concerning the unconverted in his congregation was so great that he could not sleep. He would rise in the night to pray for them, with strong cryings and tears. Occasionally he awoke his wife and asked her to sing him some pleasant hymn to soothe him to rest. In one of his anniversary sermons he referred to the kindness and sympathy shown him by his people, sending him, when prostrated by excessive labors, to the sea-side, supplying the church during his absence at their own expense. "Your unnumbered tokens and expressions of affection are not forgotten, they are laid up in my heart of hearts, and I thank God always for you, remembering you in my prayers. But all this does not satisfy, and cannot make me happy, while the cause of my Redeemer makes no more progress, and the slain of my people are so many."

In the same sermon he made a solemn appeal to the young, and alluded to the desolations which death had made during the year that was gone. "I need not tell you of him, whose lifeless body I helped, with my own hands, to raise from a distant grave, and bear to the home which he had left, in the vigor of his youth, but a little while before; nor of him who now sleeps far from the home of his childhood, where the magnolia spreads its broad petals, and the sounding waves of a southern sea sing his eternal dirge. God has been calling you in a most solemn manner, and from those new-made graves comes, in sad and reproving tones, the inquiry, 'Why sit ye here all the day idle?'"

Thus did he plead with sinners in the great congregation. On the way-side, and in the home, he urged them to be reconciled to God, and when they visited him in the Manse, he would seek a favorable opportunity of conversing and praying with them. Meeting a young woman in the church aisle, after an earnest sermon, preached by Rev. Alex. Reed, on the words of Jesus, "Seek ye first the kingdom of God and his righteousness," (Matt. vi. 33,) he addressed her in his usual kind way. "Well, A——, I trust you are seeking that kingdom." After a pastoral visit in her home, he turned to her and said, "And you, dear A——, I have been very much concerned for you." There was a peculiar solemnity and earnestness in his manner, which impressed his unconverted friend. His words kept sounding in her ears, day after day. She could not forget them. At length, through his loving faithfulness, she was brought to Jesus, and after she had entered the kingdom, his judicious counsel encouraged her fainting heart, and his kind admonitions recalled her wandering affections. Instances of this kind might be almost indefinitely multiplied. His labors were not in vain in the lord. He turned many to righteousness, and now, gone to the other world, he shall shine as a star, for ever and ever.

CHAPTER VIII.

THE PREACHER AND PASTOR.

THE duty of entire consecration to Christ was often urged upon his people. It is this which gives to the Christian life its oneness. It concentrates all our energies on the great end of being; converges all the lines of thought and action, feeling and influence, upon the glory of God. This consecration was urged by many motives drawn from this life and the next.

He pressed the importance of systematic benevolence, and practised it himself. Once he remarked: "You will allow me to say, that I act upon my faith, and am rewarded according to my faith. I have never been so happy, and never felt so certain of my daily bread, as since I commenced giving systematically to the Lord. I know God will provide for me. I have sometimes been deceived by man, but never by God. I have lost some money out of bank, but never any that I laid up in heaven. I have notes, and bonds, and mortgages, which are valueless. But here is God's word, signed, sealed, and delivered, upon which I am ready to rest my temporal comfort, and my eternal salvation." Benevolence is sure to be rewarded in this life. But the great argument was drawn from the cross of Christ:—"Ye are not your own, for ye are bought with a price."

It was gratifying to notice the growing liberality of the people. To every object of Christian benevolence that was presented, contributions were made; and as the result of the faithful instructions of the pulpit, attended with the Divine blessing, the church in Waynesburg took its position among the largest contributing churches in the Synod of Philadelphia.

Then, too, the people were stirred up to direct and personal efforts for the salvation of souls. They had failed to do their duty in this respect. "You must help me," said the pastor, "and help me more earnestly and effectually than you have done, or we cannot expect to hear the Master say, 'Well done, good and faithful servants.' When a company of men are raising a building, if nearly all cease to bear their part of the burden, it comes with a crushing weight upon a few. My dear friends, the temple of the Lord must go up. There is much work to be done. If you fail to assist, it can never be accomplished. If you will do what you can, we shall in due time bring forth the headstone, with shoutings of 'grace, grace unto it.'" The appeal had the desired effect. Much efficient aid was rendered by the session of the church. The elders were noble men; full of faith, and devoted to the interests of their Master's kingdom. Only one of these remain until the present. May the blessing of Him that dwelleth in the bush, be upon the head of that beloved man, separated for a season from his brethren!

One evening the elders were called together, and asked to undertake the visitation of the congregation. It was proposed that a district should be assigned to each, and that the pastor should follow. They acceded to the proposition without objection or hesitation. Soon after, one of them called on Mr. Thom, and invited him to attend a meeting they had appointed for prayer, that God would prepare them for their work, and aid them in it. He went with a full heart. It was a precious and memorable season. Minister and elders wept and prayed together. They prevailed with God, and it was not long until many souls were brought to Jesus. The pastor was particularly struck with the deep seriousness which he found in one of the districts, through which an elder, (R. B.,) had gone before him. This venerable and beloved servant of God felt that this was the last public work in which he would engage. The shadow of death resting upon him, he spoke with much solemnity and melting tenderness to all whom he met. Some whom he addressed, shortly after found peace in believing. In a few months the godly man laid his armor off, and, with the name of Jesus on his lips, sweetly went to his eternal rest. "Blessed are the dead which die in the Lord!"

Mr. Thom was a laborious pastor. His field was large, and it required much time to make the circuit. He found it impracticable to make many merely social visits. His attentions to the sick were prompt and unremitting, whilst the necessity for them continued. As has already been intimated, the home of affliction never waited long for his coming. He preached the gospel from house to house, and under every roof he offered many and earnest prayers. His forenoons were devoted to study, and the remainder of the day to pastoral visitation. During the six and a half years he spent in Waynesburg, there was but one Sabbath on which, when at home, he failed to preach. That was a day of much suffering and anxiety. He frequently preached when he was very unwell, and many felt like a good mother in Israel, who said, "I could not keep back the tears when I saw him entering the pulpit, knowing that he had come to it from a sick bed." His physician often advised him not to attend night meetings in bad weather, assuring him that he could not do it without positive and immediate injury to his health. He would reply, "I must work while the day lasts." This is not referred to in the way of unqualified commendation. In the judgment of his friends he often acted unwisely, and shortened his days. But it reveals the earnestness of the man, and his readiness to endure suffering for the church's sake.

A distinguished friend, who spent a season in Waynesburg, says: "More than a score of times I told him he was injuring himself; that no human being could possibly carry such a burden of labor long, and adjured him to rest. His reply, in substance, was: 'I cannot stop. The work must be done at any and all cost.' His attitude in this regard was really sublime. And yet I could wish his views of duty in the case had been different."

He was a diligent student. He was not willing to serve God with that which cost him nothing. His morning sermons were usually written, and always prepared with all the care he could bestow upon them. His afternoon sermons were unwritten. He had a decidedly metaphysical turn of mind, and was familiar with natural science. But, as a rule, his sermons were simple, and his illustrations were drawn from familiar objects in nature, and the common occurrences of life. Plain and unlettered people heard him gladly. The children could understand the most that he said, and some of them received the word with joy. He seldom took his manuscript into the pulpit, but made himself familiar with the train of thought, and for language depended, to a considerable extent, on the inspiration of the moment. His style was vigorous. He aimed at directness, rather than elegance, and yet his sermons contained many passages that could not fail to gratify the most fastidious taste.

He made a habit of reading the Scriptures in the original languages, and his Latin commentaries, with Turrettini Opera, were highly prized, and frequently consulted. The Bible and prayer were to him like the electrodes of a voltaic pile. They kept the currents of his spiritual life in motion, and prepared him to enter upon his public work with a warm heart and burning zeal. He was also fond of poetry; and astronomy, chemistry, and geology were favorite studies: but the word of God was always placed in the foreground, and through the fields of revelation he loved to range during the week, returning to his people on the Sabbath, bending under the precious fruits gathered in the spiritual vineyards of the Lord. "The Song of Songs, which is Solomon's," was to him a delightful study. Some of his sweetest and most precious sermons were suggested by the Royal Preacher, and a favorite commentary on the Song was read with a delight which continually increased.

The statement has already been made, that his preaching was often close and pungent. He believed in conviction of sin; and such doctrines as human depravity, the awful holiness of God, and the eternal punishment of the wicked, were not withheld, because distasteful to the carnal mind. Sometimes he gave such prominence to the terrors of the Lord, that many persons were thrown into great distress, and yet the outstanding characteristic of his preaching was tenderness. Especially was this the case during the last years of his ministry. Dr. M—— says: "His constant theme was Jesus; his habitual desire, the salvation of souls. In addressing his hearers, his sympathies would become so much enlisted, that it seemed he would be willing to sacrifice his own dear life, if by so doing he could bring souls to Christ. *And he did.* He died with his armor on, but being dead, he yet speaks, O, how eloquently!"

Many remember his sermon on Hebrews xii. 25, "See that ye refuse not Him that speaketh." He portrayed the sufferings of Jesus so graphically, that the cross seemed to rise to the view of the congregation, and on it hung the wounded, dying Son of God. Then he added, "O, see that ye refuse not Him that speaketh." This was repeated in a tone which thrilled his hearers. After a short pause, he continued: "Look again at that victim on the cross! Is there not a tongue in every wound, pleading with a melting tenderness which should move a heart of stone?" Then followed a beautiful portrayal of the Saviour's love to ruined men, and an appeal to hear God's own and only Son, so affectionate, that, for a moment, it seemed that no soul could leave the house of God without an entire surrender to Jesus. The love, sympathy, faithfulness, and all-sufficient grace of Christ were favorite themes. He delighted to lead his people to Calvary, sit in the shadow of the cross, contemplate the Lamb slain from the foundation of the world, and then look far above to the throne of the Lamb reigning and triumphant in heaven.

His sermons abounded in illustrations. Such is our mental and moral constitution, that deeper and more abiding impressions are made by concrete truths than by abstract statements. Hence the power of Christ's incarnation, His lowly life, and sorrowful death. We should never have known that God is love, had not that precious truth been revealed by

God manifested in the flesh. Our Saviour in His preaching adapted His style of address to the minds and hearts of men, and spake to the people in parables. Beautiful and impressive are the pictures which the Evangelists have preserved for us in the galleries of the imperishable word.

Imitating the great Teacher, Mr. Thom employed illustrations; thus conveying truth to the humblest mind, and fixing it there, as a nail in a sure place. In the sermon on the text already referred to, "see that ye refuse not Him that speaketh," the following illustrations occur. "How earnestly God calls! There is no time for delay. A party of men were raising a heavy building in the west. When almost up, a huge beam slipped from their pikes. It poised for a moment on the timbers. All saw it must fall, and there was a rush for life. But one failed to move. 'See! See!' cried his companions, as with white faces they pointed to the danger. But in vain they shouted, and shrieked the alarm. He seemed bewildered. He hesitated. 'Fly! fly! fly!' they screamed.

But still he tarried. The beam crashed down upon him, and he was dead in a moment. So hang suspended the thunderbolts of Divine vengeance. Not long will judgment linger. Not long will damnation slumber. God calls, 'See that ye refuse not Him that speaketh.'"

..... "God is always kind and good, but He has addressed mankind in very different ways. Once he came down on Mount Sinai. The mount shook; the earth trembled. In the midst of fire, and smoke, and tempest, and thunder, He uttered His voice. The man of God did exceedingly fear and quake, and the people, terror-stricken, fell to the ground. But amid all this there was no word of love. ..... Now look to the wilderness of Judea, and see a Man of Sorrows, taking upon him, at baptism, the burden of a broken law. See Him in the desert, baring His bosom to the fiery darts of Satan. Follow Him through years of toil and pain, Himself bearing our sorrows and receiving our stripes. Behold Him looking down on the devoted city, weeping as He looks. Turn your eyes to Mount Moriah.

Who is that, red from the scourging, with shame and spitting on His brow, staggering under the cross, meekly wending His way among thieves to the place of a skull, while the multitude hoot, and jeer, and scoff Him out of the world? Look again. They have pierced His hands and His feet, and hung Him on the accursed tree. His face is furrowed by the writhings of mortal agony. The powers of darkness are crowding upon Him. His father's face is turned away. He utters no word. But, look at Him! Was such pleading with sinners ever heard, as the silent pleading of that pale face and mangled form? Sit down at the foot of the cross, and look at Jesus. He is God's messenger to you. Will you now believe?"

When urging immediate flight to the cross, the only place of security for the guilty and condemned, he spake as follows: "When ascending the Alps, a traveler was thrown from his horse. He toppled over the precipice, and was dashed, a mangled corpse, upon the rocks beneath. We, too, are toiling up the

Alps. We meet with difficulties, and are obliged to labor at all times. But often we creep along the slippery verge of precipices of ruin; we cross the scarred and desolated track of the awful avalanche of passion; our feet slide on the glassy slope of glaciers of pleasure, and we tread almost unconsciously over the thin, loose covering, which conceals the pits and forges of temptation. It will not do to close our eyes. It is madness to relax our muscles. It is death to walk carelessly. Hold, then! Your feet are slipping. Drive down your steel-shod staff! Seize the hand of your Guide! Look up, lest your head grow dizzy, and you reel into the abyss! Redeem the time! Now! Now!"

Urging efforts for the salvation of others, he said: "You spring from your bed at midnight, and fly for your physician when you are wakened by symptoms of deadly disease in one of your children. The time required to bring him to the side of the little sufferer seems almost an age. Now, what would you think if he would sit coolly down and talk of the weather, and crops, and stocks, and trade, till the crisis was past, and fatal coma ensued, when all the time you knew that prompt and energetic action would save your child? You would stop him with almost savage earnestness. Bring out your hot bath! Lay on your sinapism! Force open the clenched teeth, and pour down the healing draught! Away with your business and pleasure when *life*—LIFE is trembling in the balance. 'Redeem the time.' But, my dear friends, there are deadly symptoms in the dearest child of your bosom. Sin is there, and shows itself in a thousand words, and feelings, and acts, and it needs only time to end in death. Soon the fatal stupidity will come, and all your cries will fall upon their ears unheard. Wake them from their slumber; fly to the Great Physician, and give Him no rest till He has applied the healing balm of His own blood to that precious soul!"

The following touching incident was used to illustrate the love of Christ. "In one of those sudden and terrible storms, which in the long winter sometimes burst on northern prairies, a mother was overtaken, with her little boy, miles away from home. They struggled on, but the snow was blinding, and they were pierced through with the pitiless cold. At length the stupor of approaching death began to steal upon them, but the mother's heart could not be chilled. She took the covering from her own bent shoulders, and wrapped it about the child. Then taking him in her arms she turned her back to the deadly blast, and laid herself down to die. Hours after, she was found by searching friends. She was dead! But the child, folded in her embrace, though unconscious, was yet alive. The last rays of warmth from that loving heart had been enough to save the boy. Was not that love strong as death? But what was it to the love of our Saviour, when in the storm of God's wrath, and there was no room for pity, he covered us with the robe of His righteousness, and Himself stood exposed to the vengeance which pursued Him even to death. The God-man saved us at the sacrifice of his own life!

'O, for this love let rocks and hills
Their lasting silence break!'"

In another sermon he thus discoursed on the same theme. "The love of Jesus is great. He says, 'As the Father hath loved me, so have I loved you.' How much do you love the child at your knee? Let your love be put to the test, when you are drawing him to your side, putting back the curls from his white brow, and looking down into the depths of those great eyes which are raised so wonderingly to to yours. Would you not give your life for his? . . . One of the most fearful conceptions ever cast upon the canvas is the picture of Death upon the Pale Horse, by Benjamin West. The skeleton King, bestriding a fire-breathing steed, is charging furiously over the dying and the dead. With glaring eyes, and grinding teeth, he scatters his darts on every hand. Around him, war and pestilence, wild beasts of the field and forest, fire, and lightning, and violence of every kind, are hastening on their work of destruction, and behind him come his trooping legions, and with demon claw and snaky coil they throttle the half-dead victims, and hurry them away to their torments. But just before the monster's charger sits a pale mother with her little babe, in strong convulsions, upon her bosom. While the father, forgetful of life, forgetful of pestilence, forgetful of death, forgetful of hell itself, thinking only of his first-born, writhing in his agony, casts himself before the monster and presents his own bosom to the fiery dart, or to the iron heel of the pale horse, if haply he may shield his child. The picture is true to life. It is not overdrawn. My dear friends, this is but the expression of the love of poor, imperfect, earthly beings, whose affections, as well as their other faculties, have been sadly blunted and degraded by the fall. It can but faintly shadow forth the infinite love of the Heavenly Father for his only begotten and well-beloved Son. And yet that Son, aware of all his Father's affection, says, 'As my Father hath loved me, so have I loved you.'"

As a declaimer, Mr. Thom had considerable power. He was passionately fond of listening to public speakers who excelled in oratory. He would put himself to much inconvenience, and by prodigious efforts anticipate his work, that he might hear some distinguished lecturer or elocutionist. Occasionally, as a pleasant recreation, he would entertain students, or young men of his congregation, by readings from the poets; and his rendering of stirring, pathetic, and descriptive passages from Shakspeare, Tennyson, Longfellow, and others, exhibited an unusual cultivation of voice, and command of the emotions.

Sometimes the orator was too prominent in the delivery of the sermon. Some thought him theatrical, particularly in the early part of his ministry. He rarely preached with much effect on his first appearance among strangers. The heavenly unction was wanting, to modify and soften his manner. He craved sympathy, and felt powerless without the prayers of the church. He expressed this in a letter addressed to one of his people from Bedford: "It is not so pleasant to preach away from home. Sympathy and confidence are wonderful helps to religious enjoyment. We need communion with one another, as well as with our Saviour. So, when we are away among comparative strangers, and cannot tell how far they sympathize with us, it is difficult to feel the same glow that we do when at our own altar, and among our own brethren."

At times he was truly eloquent. Professor W——, a man of much culture and superior literary attainments, writes: "The first sermon I ever heard him preach, contained several passages of great power, and one in particular, which first excited my special interest in him, and attracted my attention to him as a marked man, involving a very fine, apposite, and striking image, was as bold and happy a piece of rhetorical illustration as I ever heard or read." Similar testimony is borne in the Presbyterial Obituary: "Eloquent, simple, earnest, and abundant in illustrations, he gained the attention of the hearer, and impressed truth and duty on his heart."

He preached Christ. No matter what the subject of his sermon, he always found a natural, easy, and pleasant path to the cross. All sin was viewed in the light of Calvary. All duty was urged by motives drawn from the death of Jesus. The weak, tempted, afflicted, weary, and despondent, were directed to Him whose heart is made of tenderness; whose fulness can never be exhausted. So closely and persistently did he adhere to the precious gospel, even during those dark and memorable days of our country's trial, when our national life was imperilled, that some questioned his loyalty to the government. But on thanksgiving and fast-days, he expressed his views on the great questions of the day with so much candor and distinctness, that his patriotism could not be doubted. Even then he preached Christ the Lord. He drew an argument for devotion to the country from the life of Jesus of Nazareth, who loved His own, selected His Apostles from among His own countrymen, and commanded that the gospel should be preached in all the world, *beginning at Jerusalem.* Then he urged submission to the *Lord,* who ordains the powers that preside over the nation. Content with such expressions of sentiment on these set occasions, he devoted the rest of his time to preaching the simple, essential truths of religion. The sanctuary was a quiet retreat from the noise and turmoil which continued through the week, and on the Sabbath the attention of dying men and women was directed to the unseen world, and the kingdom which endureth for ever. By this course, quiet and harmony were continued in the church. Whilst many other congregations were distracted and rent, not a single family or individual withdrew from his, and out of the fiery trial the church came forth at last, strong, and as united, as before the war.

In all his labors, he endeavored to keep the glory of God continually in view. He had conflicts, such as are common to men. Love of applause, natural ambition, and self-love, often troubled him. He needed to watch and pray. But nothing could have induced him to turn aside from the ministry, and that Christ might be glorified in him and by him, was the habitual and controling desire of his life. To a mercenary minister, who once made an offensive proposition, he said, with much feeling, and some indignation: "If this day I should be offered the income I once had, (as a teacher at Natchez, which was at least three times greater than his salary as pastor,) and all the ease it is possible to enjoy, on condition that I turn aside from the service of God in the ministry, I would not look at it for a moment." At another time, a warm personal friend, who was wealthy and advanced in life, wished him to take ten thousand dollars, asking only the legal interest for the same during the remainder of his life. Some of his friends advised him to accept the offer, but after a little consideration he declined it: "I was afraid it was a temptation of the devil."

Whilst teaching at Natchez, he accumulated a considerable sum of money. The first thing he did, was to return four-fold to a sister, who had assisted him to secure his collegiate education. He also gave to the support of his father, and the education of his younger sisters. What remained, after meeting personal expenses, was invested in the South. This was all lost during the war. Yet he never murmured, and the shadow of distrust in God never crossed his mind. But few knew of the loss he had sustained. To an intimate friend he remarked: "If our country is saved, my property shall be a most cheerful offering: if the government is overthrown, it would have been of no use to me." To his wife he said: "I have not a doubt but that we will be provided for. I have laid all on God's altar, and His promise is sure."

Writing from Atlantic City, whither he had gone to recruit his health, he says: "I am now much improved, and I hope I shall get entirely well. O, if God would be pleased to make me strong again, I would be thankful. There is so much I want to do for Him. I do think my heart's desire and prayer to God is, that His name may be glorified, and souls saved through me."

And thus, seeking submission to God's will in all things, glorying only in the cross of Christ, through disappointment, affliction, and weariness, he held on his way, and many believed on Jesus through his word.

CHAPTER IX.

ADDITIONAL CHARACTERISTICS.

He was a man of remarkable charity. Going back to his early youth we find the following in his diary. "I have been schooling myself to think well of men, when it is possible, and not to speak ill of any one. To a degree I have succeeded: but my heart is often full of bitterness. O! meek and lowly Jesus, give me of Thy Spirit!" An intimate friend in later years, says, "I never heard him utter an uncharitable remark." Another, who knew him well, says; "He was a man of the largest charity. I never heard him express an ill feeling or an unfriendly sentiment with reference to any human being, and *that* although our conversation often fell upon men whose views and practices were diametrically opposite to his own. He had no jealousies. He used to recount the merits and excellencies of his brethren in the ministry, with whom he would naturally be compared, with the most evident pleasure, deeming their successes his own."

His self-forgetfulness was great. Where duty pointed, he went, no matter what toil or suffering lay in the way. He bore other men's burdens, he forgot his need of rest, and night vigils with the sick and dying were continued beyond the ordinary limits of human endurance. To reward merit, he would put himself on the background. To promote a friend, he would humble himself. To relieve suffering, he would sacrifice personal comfort. These are statements confirmed by the observation of all, and by the experience of many, who knew him.

He was a patient sufferer. Afflicted much of his life, he seldom spoke of his bodily ailments. Often when racked with severe pain, he went through all his usual Sabbath services, or visited his people, and his calm, cheerful manner, suggested no inquiries concerning his health. He would refer with much feeling to the afflictions of friends, and bear his own in patient silence.

His genial hospitality will be gratefully remembered by many. His ministerial friends always received a most cordial welcome. The invalid stranger, lacking needed comforts at the village hotel, has found a home in the minister's family, kindly watched and cared for, and sent on his way with pleasant memories that shall never die. "I was a stranger," says one, who soon learned to love him, "and he took me in. I came from a distant part of the country; he never seemed for a moment to feel the slightest local prejudice, but hailed and welcomed me among his people and to his own fire-side, with protracted and free hospitality, and most generous attentions, so long as my continuance required or admitted."

He was wont to enter readily and heartily, and with great self-forgetfulness, into all the hopes, wishes and anxieties of all who appealed to him, or whom he saw in need of sympathy or aid.

He was delicate in giving counsel. His sensibilities were acute; his tact ready, and his appreciation of the whole case presented, was wonderfully complete. His advice to the soul, burdened with sin, was judicious. He rarely bewildered with much talking, but by a few appropriate words, met the case, and relieved the anxiety.

He was peculiarly happy in addressing the afflicted and bereaved. He urged them with a sweet persuasiveness to carry their burdens to Jesus; contrasted the light afflictions with the glory to be revealed; turned their thoughts to the rest of that world where clouds shall never gather, and sorrow shall never come. There are bereaved ones on their way home to-day, whose pathway will be brightened to its close by the remembrance of his sympathy, and the comforting words he spake.

He had a rare capacity for joy and suffering. This being the case, he was peculiarly careful of others, placing himself between them and suffering, physical or mental, whenever it was possible. He was mindful of the Divine direction: "Bear ye one another's burdens, and so fulfil the law of Christ." Gal. vi. 2.

His social qualities were of a high order. He eschewed the cold formality of fashionable life. He was natural, warm, and free in intercourse with his friends, and won the churlish by his courteous and kind attentions.

He was preëminently a man of prayer. When oppressed, wounded, fearful, discouraged, happy, he went to the "secret place of the stairs." He had stated times for private devotions, and studiously guarded against any interruption or diversion from them. He always rose early, in order that he might secure time for devotional reading, meditation, and prayer. He carried every want to Jesus. The daily cares of the family were laid before the Heavenly Friend, and direction sought in all the plans which had reference to his domestic duties and enjoyments. One day, when his wife was perplexed about certain provisions for the household, he said, "Did you ask God for it?" "Do you ask for such things?" "Yes, always. Everything I think it right to desire

I ask for, believing that if it is best I should have it, God would give it."

He disliked late hours. Saturday evening he wanted to himself. Often he failed to secure time for meditation and prayer on that evening, by reason of the interruption of visitors. Then the night was apt to be one of restlessness, and often, on his bed, he was overheard pleading for a blessing upon his people and himself.

His love to Christians was strong. He often spoke with great affection of some of his friends who were eminent for piety. His heart warmed toward the humblest who bore the image of the Saviour. As he grew more like Jesus, his love toward the weakest disciple increased. Of one he writes: "C—— is a good man, a noble man, a thinking man, and, better than all, a praying man. I derive much advantage from his society." Of another, to whom his soul was knit, as David's to Jonathan: "There is no man I ever saw that comes nearer to my idea of a good man than

E——," and he loved him because he walked with God.

He loved to converse on subjects pertaining to Christ and his kingdom. The writer remembers talks about Jesus, when walking with him through the fields, or sitting together in the quiet study. His face would brighten as he dwelt on the beauties of the Beloved, the One altogether lovely, and his eyes would fill with tears as he spoke of the way by which the kind Shepherd had led him. There was a sick minister who spent several days in his family. He was one who had lived near the cross, and breathed the atmosphere of heaven on earth. "I love Jesus, and I like to tell him so," the minister was wont to say. Very pleasant were the conversations between the sufferer and his tender nurse, and during those few days they were bound together by bonds of Christian affection, which even death has not sundered. There was no spiritual parade manifested in his conversation. He avoided the appearance of religious cant. He was never attracted to persons who talked religion on all occasions, and honored Christ but little, if at all, by Christian labors. "Some people's tongues are larger than both their hands." But with simple-minded and sincere Christians he held sweet counsel, and was greatly refreshed by it. His views on "Religious Conversation" were fully presented in an elaborate and eminently practical article, written several years ago, and published in a monthly magazine. It was based on the words of the prophecy, Malachi iii. 16. He insisted that if Jesus was oftener the subject of devout and loving contemplation we would oftener talk about Him. "While I was musing, the fire burned: then spake I with my tongue." Psalm xxxix. 3.

He was a cheerful Christian, equally removed from levity and moroseness. At *times* he was very sad. His tender sympathies and warm affections made him a sufferer. But he was *habitually* cheerful. He had strong faith in the Covenant-God, and believed all things would work together for his good. He thought the Christian had much to be thankful for, and abiding ground for hope. "Let the children of Zion be joyful in their King." When he walked or rode abroad with a friend, and, with his ardent love of nature, talked of the grandeur of the mountains, or the beauties of the valleys, he found an argument for joy in all that he saw, recalling the beautiful lines of the pious Cowper:

> "He looks abroad into the varied field
> Of nature, and though poor perhaps, compared
> With those whose mansions glitter in his sight,
> Calls the delightful scenery all his own.
> His are the mountains, and the valleys his,
> And the resplendent rivers. His to enjoy
> With a propriety that none can feel,
> But who with filial confidence inspired,
> Can lift to heaven an unpresumptuous eye,
> And smiling, say—' My Father made them all.'"

And yet he was subject to seasons of religious depression, and was often distressed by the fierce and protracted assaults of Satan. He records his conflicts with the adversary, and his attempts to escape from his snares. "I read Hebrew, I read theology, I write sermons, but I can neither read nor write myself clear of the Gorgons which meet me at every turn." His only relief was found in looking to Jesus. He is the Lord, strong and mighty in battle. To Him he carries his despondency and fear. By and by the dark clouds all roll away, and the heavens are full of glory. "I feel that I love Jesus, and am loved by Him." Then, after a season of great religious enjoyment, depression comes again, and Satan, taking advantage of the exhaustion induced by excessive joy, renews his attacks, and the buffetted soul realizes that unbroken rest is not to be found on this side of the grave. Sometimes he would waken his wife, far on in the night, and say, "My dear, come to me, I am in the dark. I cannot find Him." He had spent nearly all the night in agonizing prayer for the light of God's face. Then his wife would go to him, tell him of the faithfulness of Jesus, take him by the hand, as if he were a little child, and lead him to the cross. The night of weeping was succeeded by a morning of joy.

There was a pious widow near by, to whom he would sometimes go in his seasons of depression, and was often lifted up by her large and loving experience. She had been in the fires. Her husband had gone home to God, and left her alone with Jesus. She had learned precious lessons in the night of sorrow, and had the tongue of the learned to speak words of comfort to this weary, burdened one. Refreshed by christian converse, he would say: "Though He slay me, yet will I trust in Him. I will rejoice in the Lord, and joy in the God of my salvation. My Saviour! My Saviour! He died for me—on the cross!"

One day he left his study, and passed into an adjoining room that he might tell his wife he was again in the dark, and ask her to pray for him. One of his children, then three years old, was playing on the floor. Whether he comprehended what his father was saying, cannot certainly be told. But presently he began to sing,

> "O, do not be discouraged,
> For Jesus is your Friend,"

and having sung the sweet couplet, went on with his play. His father was moved to tears, and went away to cast himself on the tender compassion of the Friend who was born for adversity.

Physical causes had doubtless much to do with these seasons of despondency. "It is mine infirmity" which often beclouds the mind, and almost crushes out our hope. His friend, the Rev. Dr. Plumer, whom he loved as a father, comprehended the case, and after listening to a sad narration of his experiences, through the darkest months of his life, the good Doctor said: "The trouble is with the physical. It is worn out. You need rest. The question is, how to get it." It is a pleasant thought that physical disorders are unknown in heaven, and no clouds ever cast a shadow over the soul that out of tribulation has gone thither.

We close this chapter with a paragraph written by one who was, for many years, one of Mr. Thom's most familiar friends. "There was a childlike simplicity in his (Mr. T's) christian character, which those unacquainted with him would not appreciate. I often thought, in conversations with him on the subject of experimental religion, that his views were singularly clear on the great saving truths of the gospel. With simple, yet strong faith, he clung to Christ as his Saviour, and showed an earnest desire to be more and more transformed into his likeness. I now recall with melancholy pleasure the many Sabbath evenings I spent with him at the Seminary, when in christian confidence we spoke to each other of our inner life. I love to think of him, and of my intercourse with him. And while with gratitude I recall the past, faith points forward to the time when I hope that the sacred and delightful communings of earth shall be renewed in heaven."

CHAPTER X.

THE HUSBAND AND FATHER.

Philip Henry was wont to say: "A good Christian will be a good father, and a good husband, and a good master, and a good neighbor, and so in other relations." He was undoubtedly right. One who was questioned as to his christian integrity, referred the inquirer to his family for the desired information. There are many professors of religion who fail to exhibit the beauties of holiness in their homes. It was otherwise with Mr. Thom. Nowhere did he manifest the graces of the Spirit more fully than in his family. He did not need to be reminded of the apostolic injunction: "Husbands love your wives." A more affectionate, considerate, self-forgetful, devoted husband, the writer never knew. No one could spend a day in his family without being impressed with his loving attentions to his wife and children, and the spirit of piety which characterized every word and act.

His was a happy home. The little house, removed from the dusty highway, sheltered by trees, overshadowed too by vigilant love, and surrounded by the ministering spirits sent from the Father above, well deserved the designation of "Sunny Side."

One who spent some time in the manse says, he never before had seen the christian graces so manifested in any household, and that during his sojourn in it, influences for good were brought about him, "stronger than hooks of steel."

Mr. Thom was very attentive to the little things of life; little acts of kindness, expressions of affection, and the like. Perhaps no wife ever received more constant and delicate attentions than his. It was his joy to carry her burdens. Often, when weary with the labors of the day, he insisted that he would watch with the sick children through the night, in order that her rest might be undisturbed.

The first years of his married life were years of much affliction. He said there was a necessity for these afflictions. They were evidently blessed to his spiritual good, and enlarged his sympathies with the afflicted. God's ministers endure much suffering for their people's sake. "Blessed be God, even the Father of our Lord Jesus Christ, the Father of mercies, and God of all comfort; who comforteth us in all our tribulation, that we may be able to comfort them which are in any trouble, by the comfort wherewith we ourselves are comforted of God."

When his first-born son was less than a year old, he was taken very sick. For weeks and even months, it was feared the child would not recover. The father was greatly depressed, as he sat, day after day, in the shadow of an oncoming sorrow which no human hand could avert. To his wife he said, with a tone of regretfulness: "Instead of bearing you up, my dear, I am leaning on you, like a tired child: but I never was so completely unmanned." At length he was enabled, in calm submission, to give his child to God, and then God gave back the child to him. He rose from that baptism of fire, enfeebled in body, but with a new consecration to God, who had afflicted him in love.

Soon after this, his wife was prostrated by violent sickness. Through weeks of anxiety, he could scarcely eat or sleep. His attentions were constant. God brought her back from the gates of the grave, and they magnified the name of the Lord together. Those months of almost sleepless anxiety, to one of his impulsive, ardent temperament, told unmistakably on the physical man, and no sooner was the stress of high-wrought feeling relaxed, than the overtaxed strength went rapidly down. Then followed the death of his father. "The clouds return after the rain."

He endeavored to make the home attractive to his children. Beautiful engravings, and oil paintings, decorated the walls. He devised healthful and pleasant amusements for the children, and so varied them, as to prevent weariness. He amused and instructed his boys by anecdotes, of which he had an inexhaustible store, by the rehearsal of incidents in his own life, and by telling them of beautiful scenes he had witnessed in his distant journeyings. Then he had many pleasant talks with them about Jesus, the children's friend, and endeavored to turn their hearts to Him in the morning of life.

When weary and worn with pastoral labors, returning late in the day from long rides, and perhaps with some burden on his heart, he often said, "Nothing so takes the tired out of me, as the welcome I receive from my wife and boys." His physician, who was present one evening, having witnessed the joy of the children on their father's return, remarked: "a parent cannot come home to such a scene, and keep very gloomy thoughts. The sound of baby voices, the touch of little hands climbing at the knees, must surely drive anxious care away." To a great extent it was so in the experience of the father to whom the remark was addressed.

On one occasion, when absent, his eldest boy

endeavored to comfort his mother, and said he would take his father's place. She inquired if he could not ask God to bring his father to him. He turned aside, lifted his hands, and said: "Please God, bring papa home to mamma and Bertie," and then added—"God heard Bertie's voice." The father came home to spend a few days with the family, but received no welcome from his boy, who was then very sick, and in his delirium failed to recognize his parent, and would not consent to his entering the room. This affected Mr. Thom very deeply, and he could not refrain from tears. The following day he succeeded in quieting the child, and took the little sufferer in his arms, who, after looking long and inquiringly in the father's face, recognized him, and putting his arms around his neck, repeated over and over again his expressions of love. The father wept again, but now for joy. This incident shows the strong bond of sympathy which united the father and his child, and the depth of the parent's affection.

When absent, his thoughts were so much

given to his family, and he felt so concerned for their comfort, that he did not derive the advantage from his occasional vacations which he needed. In one of his letters to his wife occurs the following expressions of solicitude for her health, "Your system, too long excited, shows the effects of over-exertion. Remember your life and health are not yours alone. Another heart bleeds in every throb of pain you feel. Another spirit looks for happiness to that which animates you. Your life is a double one, and its mission double."

His success in controlling his children was remarkable. From early infancy his authority was undisputed, and yet he was gentle and indulgent. He ruled by love. The times for family worship were so arranged that all might be present, and he endeavored to make the service attractive, never wearisome. In addition to the family devotions, he made a habit of offering a special prayer for the boys, after they had retired at night. The family devotions in the evening, were always observed, for the children's sake, immediately after the evening meal, and at a later hour the parents again committed themselves and little ones to the care of the covenant-keeping God. Truly could the father say, "Seven times a day do I praise thee, because of thy righteous judgments."

One evening, after he had prayed with his wife, being in one of those pensive moods which sometimes came over him when he thought of his children, he turned to his wife, and said: "Dear, I don't want you to die, and leave me with the care of these boys. Who could manage those dispositions, that require such peculiar care and prudence, so well as you. A father never can keep little children with him, a mother, no matter what her circumstances, always can." These twilight moments were among the sweetest and most sacred in the lives of those parents; moments when they looked forward and on into eternity, their hearts knit lovingly together as they talked of their little ones, and in arms of faith committed them to Him who has said, "I will be a God unto thee, and to thy seed after thee."

His faith in the God of the Covenant was usually strong. To the mother he would often say, "Keep near the cross." When she was depressed he would ask her to cast her burden on the Lord, and trust in his word. "You lean on me with perfect confidence. You know how much I love that perfect trust. You tell me I have never abused it, and earth affords me no greater joy than to hear you say so. Just so Christ would have you, in perfect confidence, lean on Him. You are weak. Tell Him so. He offers you His strength. Trust in Him; He loves to have you do it." Thus he threw light on the dark places, and helped his wife to lean on Him, "on whom archangels lean."

He frequently wrote to his children when absent from them. Here is a specimen. "Good morning! two boys! How are you this morning? Are you good boys, and kind to your dear mother, and do you pray every day for me? I am down by the big sea. Sometimes I see great fishes: one day a porpoise, one day a shark; and I often see little fishes, herring, and flounders, and it is fine sport to catch them. Can you tell me of any one the Bible tells about, who went a fishing? Now, my sweet boys, go and play, and be kind to one another, and may God bless you."

Speaking of the separation from his family, when in a western city, he says: "Enjoyment is not enjoyment without you, my dear suffering wife. God bless you and our sweet babes. . . . . But dearest, I know we meet at the feet of Jesus. I know our elder Brother watches over us. If I could not commend you to a covenant-keeping God, what should I do? Now, my dear wife, my heart is yearning after you and our dear boys. What homesick desires I feel, as I count the days that keep me from you. . . . . . God bless you, my love, and God bless our dear babes, and bring me safe home, to be separated as seldom as His blessed will may allow."

Referring to the brief seasons which, unoccupied with pastoral duties, were spent in the home-circle, he says: "Those pleasant moments shed their light backward and forward, till all my life looks bright for them."

CHAPTER XI.

MISCELLANEOUS LETTERS.

His letters were necessarily written, as a rule, "currente calamo"—with a running pen, for he was greatly pressed with labor. They are not specimens of fine writing, but simple, and often touching, utterances of the heart. They are eminently spiritual. As he made it a rule to speak to fellow-travelers on the subject of personal religion, so also to write many things "touching the King." His correspondence is fragrant with the name of Jesus, and breathes the spirit of one who lived in habitual communion with God.

It would be well if Christians more frequently availed themselves of the opportunities furnished, in the interchange of letters, of doing good to one another, and of pressing Christ upon the acceptance of their unconverted friends. In this way, precious seed might be silently deposited in many minds, and only the harvest-time of eternity would reveal the fruitfulness of such essays to do good. Why should there not be something in every letter of friendship, which shall point to the future world, and to Him who is the way to the Father?

For reasons already given, Mr. Thom's correspondence was not very extensive. From the few letters which have come into our possession we select such as may be most profitable to the reader, and exhibit the different phases of his Christian character.

From Natchez, he writes thus to a friend: "This is a beautiful world! The sweetest birds and the loveliest flowers, the rarest perfumes, and the clearest sky, are around me and above me. All nature is rejoicing in the full bloom of spring, and such a spring, to a native of a more northern climate, is astonishing, and the luxuriance and prodigality of nature here cannot be conceived without being seen. It is just now the season of roses, and every garden, lawn, and even every hedgerow, is a wilderness of fragrance and beauty. How can any one be sad in such a paradise? Truly, God is good. But, alas! the curse is upon it all.

> 'Every prospect pleases,
> And only man is vile.'"

After his arrival at Princeton, September 10, 1857: "I have closed my engagements at the south. I have bid adieu to friends more endeared than I had hoped to find in the land of strangers. With many a heart-throb I spoke the oft repeated farewell, and almost wept when the fervent 'God bless you,' fell on my ear. I climbed the great father of waters to where 'La belle reviere' mingles its clear waters in the turbid flood. I swept across the great prairies, once the hunting ground of the Indian, and the pasture of his companion, the bison. I visited the Queen City, climbed her observatory hill, and gazed upon the sweltering thousands beneath; traversed the plains of Ohio, smiling with cultivation, and rejoicing in abundant har-

vests; stopped amid the smoke and soot of
Pittsburgh, to revive the most delightful associations man is privileged to enjoy—those of
friendship and affection; mounted the Alleghenies, breathed the pure mountain air, and
rejoiced in the untouched tokens of God's
power; passed through the valleys, and
among the hills of southern Pennsylvania, and
Maryland; climbed the Washington monument in Baltimore, and looked upon the city,
its crowded streets, magnificent buildings,
elegant monuments, the bay covered with
sails, like white sea-birds floating in the distance, the country beyond stretching away
like the vanishing creations of a dream;
passed through the cedar groves of Maryland,
then away to the capitol, then to Mt. Vernon,
thence to the Quaker City, and New York;
back again to my home, a few hours of repose,
a few of enjoyment, a few of travel, and here I
am, in the school of prophets, sitting at the feet
of the doctors of theology, in the same room
where Alexander and Miller taught young
men the great principles of the gospel! O

Spirit of the past, if yet lingering about these walls, inspire me with zeal to pursue in the footsteps of the worthies who have gone before! And O! Spirit of the living God, breath into my soul the inspiration Thou alone canst give."

"Princeton, Feb. 1, 1858. I have sent to Philadelphia for a ticket to 'Everett's Washington Oration.' They were all disposed of before any were publicly offered for sale. Tickets are now selling for three dollars, which at first cost fifty cents. What a position for a man to occupy! To see a whole city contending for the privilege of even standing to hear him declaim a piece he has already declaimed nearly seventy times! I would rather be Everett than emperor of all the Russias, and yet he that is least in the kingdom of heaven is greater than he."

To an afflicted friend: "Two days ago you were trembling with apprehension. Are you now weeping with bereaved tenderness? or giving thanks for the removal of His rod? Shall I say, 'whom the Lord loveth He chasteneth?' or 'The Lord is merciful and gracious, slow to anger, and of tender mercies?' I can say both, and more—'Trust in the Lord, and be of good courage. The Lord will give grace and glory.' The first time we ever talked together, we spoke of the wonderful adaptation of God's consolations in His word to the wants of the human heart. We both, I trust, know far more of them now. Let us thank Him for all His mercies, of which, strength to endure to this time, and the promise of strength to endure unto the end, are by no means the smallest. Let us pray to be strong in the Lord, and in the power of His might."

To another in affliction: "I am sorry you are so unwell this summer. I think I can sympathize with you better now than ever before. God always intends some good when he afflicts us. He desires to make us holier, happier, or more useful in this world, and to work out for us a far more exceeding and eternal weight of glory in the world to come. That is what makes this life worth living for—

the world to come! O! what a blessed thing it will be to be there, and count over all God's mercies, some of them in the form of afflictions, but all of them mercies still. Some of them dark and mysterious, but all good. Let us trust Him ever, and He will make plain what now is dark."

To a dear friend, whose home-circle had been entered by death, he writes expressions of tenderest sympathy and words of comfort: "Your letter of January 1st came to-day: that sad, sad letter, with the black seal. And can it be that she has lain so many weeks in the cold grave? .... And that poor boy! A sad picture comes before me, painted not on the memory, but on the heart, when I too wept my baby tears at a desolate fireside. And O! if that were all! If the first burst of childish grief could remove the shadow from the heart! But *that* darkens and darkens. Poor little orphan boy! May God take thee up! And then, too, your poor brother! I see him yet, as I saw him kissing the cold lips of his firstborn son, and I know, O! how well I know, the strong agony which the rod wrings from the bruised heart, when we see our homes blasted, and our hopes of love and happiness all swept away in a moment. We kiss the rod with a quivering lip, and with tremulous voice and broken, we cry, 'Father, Thy will be done.' Tell your brother that away in this far country, there is one heart that shares in the sorrow that grows up from *her* grave, and joins in the earnest cry, 'lead us to the Rock that is higher than we.' The Lord hear him in the day of trouble; the name of the God of Jacob defend him, send him help from the sanctuary, and strengthen him out of Zion."

When at the Seminary, having heard of the sickness of a student, an entire stranger, Mr. Thom proposed sitting up with him, and was taken to the sick room by a friend. He succeeded in soothing the nervous sufferer who remarked, some time in the night, that he had not felt so comfortable in a long time, and in the morning begged his kind nurse to return. Mr. Thom was glad to do anything in his power to alleviate suffering, and he remained with the young man until he was "carried home by the angels." He alludes to this case in the following letter. "This silent, solitary chamber; the stillness that reigns over a hundred sleepers; the adjacent bed of death; the melancholy tale of him who died alone, with no tenderer hand than a fellow-student's to close his eyes—all cast a gloom over this dark and stormy night, fit emblem of the night of life, through which we poor pilgrims are so wearily and doubtfully groping our way: But the dawn lies beyond. 'He shall a pure and heavenly spirit be,' when the sufferings and neglect of life are forgotten. For many years the grave has demanded its annual tribute from this institution. One, every session, bequeathes his uncompleted labor to his fellows, and goes to present himself as a kind of first-fruits at the great sanctuary above. Whose turn will it be next?..... You, too, wrote almost from the chamber of death. And is your dear friend in the General Assembly above? The fathers, where are they? and the prophets, do they live for ever?"

We have already referred to his interest in young men. It was a great pleasure to him to write to students, and others, who had gone out from his congregation, and *they* were equally pleased to regard him as their pastor still, though far removed from their spiritual home. To one he writes,

"January 6, 1862. Dear W——, I was glad to receive your letter. I never forget my friends, and especially my people, and above all, the young men of my charge. It is pleasant to feel that I in turn am not forgotten. I can sympathize very readily with you as I was once a παῖδαγωγος. I like the term very well: much better than the Latin *ludimajester*, though your teachers at M—— combine the meaning of both in a high degree. To excel in leading youth both in literature and athletics, merits no small praise. I am not at all sorry that you sometimes feel the annoyances and burden of teaching, as well as the pleasures. They are as necessary to give you moral muscle, as foot-ball and cricket are to give you physical. But there is a higher kind of muscle, if I may use the term, brought out by groans and tears, wrung from us by trials and agony. Trials are as needful for our spiritual health, as exercise for the bodily. They are necessary for our religious usefulness also. I doubt much whether any man was ever able to get hold of the deep-seated passions, and springs of human action, whose own soul was never refined in the crucible...... Don't say you would rather suffer something else than what God lays upon you. He knows best. And as a physician prescribes the most healing nostrum without regard to its taste, and often because it is bitter and sickening, so God often makes us suffer till our soul is in bitterness, to bring health and happiness afterward."

Again he addresses two young men:—
"Dear friends, I write to both of you together, for you seem very much like brothers, and members of my own family. Some time ago, I received a circular from A——, asking me to dismiss you to join the college church. I feel a little as a father does, when he bids good-

bye to his boy who is going out to return no more. I have all the while felt that, though you were away, you belonged to me. But it may be better you should unite with the church there. I leave it to your own judgment, and if you think it best, present the enclosed certificate, and be received at as early a day as you can.

"But, my dear friends, remember that you are anywhere, and everywhere, members of the body of Christ, and temples of the Holy Ghost, and see that you keep yourselves holy for His sacred service. The temple of the Lord is holy, which temple ye are."

We will close with a letter written from Bedford. "Dear Mrs. L——, I have been traveling every day since I left Waynesburg, except Sabbath, through the mountains and through the valleys, until I am quite glad to sit still for a few days. This is a beautiful region, and I am much refreshed by seeing and becoming acquainted with brethren in the ministry.

"I saw Mr. B—— at H——. Spent a

couple of hours with him, in a mixture of sad and pleasing emotions. His expectations of labor, and even life, are extremely low. But I cannot say he is cast down. He lays hold, with the strength of Israel, on the Angel of the Covenant. O! how he does talk. I could only listen, with my heart in my throat, and my hands over my face. But I thank God there are such consolations in religion. For a a man in the vigor of life, with high prospects of usefulness and reputation before him, to sink into silence, and drag out the rest of his years without aim or hope, is hard. But, to see all this done cheerfully, thankfully, is glorious! It makes one think more of the light afflictions which are but for a moment, working out for us a far more exceeding and eternal weight of glory. I feel the better for my tears. May God give us grace always to lean on Him!

"I have met an unusual number of friends and acquaintances of other years. The sight of them takes me back to the times when life was but little of what it is now."

He refers to the want of comfort in preaching to strange congregations, and continues: "As the home-feeling grows, my comfort at home, and my want of comfort away, increases. Last Sabbath we celebrated the Lord's Supper. We had a precious time, and the Master of the feast seemed very near. How strange, when His presence is so sweet, that we should grow cold, and grieve Him away again. . . . . Pray for me, and for the whole church; for me, that I may return strong in the Lord, and find you all baptized with the same blessed Spirit."

CHAPTER XII.

CHAPLAIN IN THE ARMY.

As a result of excessive labors and domestic afflictions, during the third year of his ministry, Mr. Thom's health was so much impaired, that his congregation urged him to take a vacation of six weeks or two months, and made provision for the pulpit during his absence. He went to Bedford, expecting to derive much benefit from the pure mountain air, and the mineral waters, which attract so many invalids to that pleasant region. He had been there but a short time when he received a telegram, informing him that his father was dangerously ill. He started immediately for Eldersridge, to which place his father had removed several years before. He arrived there a few hours previous to the death of his venerable parent, and by encouraging words and fervent prayers, brought comfort to the aged christian in his last moments.

This was during the dark days of our national history, when the deep foundations of the government were shaken, and brother met brother in sanguinary conflict. At this particular time our army needed reinforcements, and Mr. Thom was among the "drafted men." Hearing of this, he returned to Waynesburg. He would not allow his congregation to pay the commutation which would have released him from military service, neither would he accept a substitute. There were reasons for this course, which he deemed providential, and imperatively binding. It was a great trial, but he met it with an unwavering resolution.

The day before the drafted men left home was communion Sabbath. It seemed to every one that an impenetrable cloud hung over the assembled congregation. There was a death-like silence, and unwonted solemnity, through all the hours of worship. At the close of the service the pastor made his announcements. He told the people no man had more to live for than he, and yet he thought no man was more willing to lay down his life for his country, when God called for the sacrifice. His, perhaps, was the only calm face in the congregation. The next morning "he went with the men" to West Chester, the designated rendezvous. Very unexpectedly, and to the great joy of his family and people, he was released from military duty, and permitted to return home. But all this painful experience was yet a preparation for another trial which was not far distant.

An incident illustrative of his sympathy with the suffering, may be fitly introduced in this connection. In the early part of the next winter, one of the young men of the congregation, then connected with the army, died in a hospital near Fredericksburg, Virginia. He was the son of a widow, and his father was one of the godly elders who, not long before, had gone to his peaceful rest. An unavailing effort had been made by an only brother to secure the remains of the deceased soldier. The grief of the family was very great. Then, with his characteristic self-forgetfulness, Mr. Thom proposed to render whatever assistance he could, to bring home the dead. He went with the brother to Washington City. There he found it impossible to get the necessary passes. The army was expected to move within a few days, and if the body was ever to be recovered, immediate effort must be made. Through the kindness of Rev. Dr. Gurley, Mr. Thom was sent within the army lines as a representative of the Christian Commission. He had made no arrangements for a lengthened absence from home, and was illy prepared for unavoidable exposure in that inclement season. It was mid-winter, and the season was peculiarly unfavorable. With an unpleasant prospect before him he started alone. He suffered much from cold and fatigue, and it was several months before he recovered from the exposure of those anxious weeks. He succeeded in his errand, and to-day the body of the noble young soldier sleeps with his fathers, in the family burial-ground.

While with the army, at this time, we are

told that Mr. Thom ministered with "womanly tenderness" to the temporal and spiritual wants of the soldiers, and doubtless the fruits of that service have, as yet, been but partially gathered.

When in a measure recovered from the indisposition which followed this labor of love, he accepted an invitation to spend a week in Bedford. The church in that place was enjoying a revival of religion, and the pastor, who up to that time had labored alone, needed assistance. For a few days Mr. Thom preached with considerable difficulty, and but little freedom. His physical condition had an unfavorable effect on his spiritual state, at least so far as concerned the enjoyment of public religious services. He felt that he was only declaiming, not preaching. It grieved and humbled him. After a day of great depression and much prayer, he went to the evening meeting with a feeling of utter helplessness, clinging to the sufficient grace of Christ. He preached a very simple and impressive sermon. It was an affectionate presentation of the truth concerning the Lamb of God, and souls were drawn to the embrace of the Saviour's love. From that time onward, during his stay in Bedford, he preached in demonstration of the Spirit and with power. Very sweet was the communion with the Beloved, and the joy of that harvest-time shall never be forgotten.

From Bedford he returned home, with a heart all aglow with love to Christ and souls. After the warm welcome from his family, he called his wife aside, and requested that she would not oversee the "special dinner," nor do anything else, until he had told her what the Lord was doing for the people among whom he had labored? Then, with a beaming countenance and full heart, he spake of the revival, and the precious communings enjoyed with Jesus; after which they knelt together at the mercy-seat, "where friend holds fellowship with friend," and in a fervent prayer he commended the church in Bedford, and their pastor, to the Heavenly Friend, who has said, "Lo, I am with you alway." The influence of that visit lingered with him through many months. He preached to his people with unusual unction and power, and his own advance in the Divine life was continuous and joyous.

At a later period he preached for a brief season at Coleraine, Pennsylvania. The pastor, Rev. C. W. Stewart, gives his personal impressions of those services: "It seemed to me that Mr. Thom, at this time, was fast ripening for heaven. There was an indefinable something about his manner that impressed me deeply. He seemed to be overwhelmed with a sense of responsibility as a minister of the gospel, and preached as I had never heard him preach before. He seemed to feel that he was preaching to us for the last time, and told us that he would soon stand as a witness, for or against us, at the bar of God. In the evening of our communion Sabbath he preached a sermon to the unconverted, which made a powerful impression upon our people. During the great revival in our church, a month or two later, there were many who dated their serious impressions from that solemn discourse."

The summer of 1863 was a memorable season in the history of this country. Then the southern army, under General Lee, crossed the Potomac, and invaded Pennsylvania. It was the culmination of rebellion, and the darkest hour in all the long years of the cruel war. Many despaired of saving the nation from utter overthrow, and proposed a cessation of hostilities. A larger number were determined to repel the invading armies, or perish in the attempt. One day a telegram was received at Waynesburg, stating that the bridge at Columbia, Pennsylvania, had been burned, in order to check the progress of the enemy, then gathered in considerable force at Wrightsville, on the opposite side of the river. That night the village bells were rung, and the people of Waynesburg and vicinity were assembled to consider their duty to the country in this alarming emergency. Mr. Thom addressed them in a very eloquent appeal to defend their native state, their homes, and all that was dear to them, pledging himself to go with any who would offer themselves for military service.

Chiefly through his influence, a full company was raised. Mr. T. G. Buchanan, a member of his congregation, was elected captain of the company, and Mr. Thom took his place in the ranks as a private soldier. Very sad was the parting from his family, but brushing away the tears, and commending his wife and boys to the care of Him who is always near, he went forth to meet the uncertain issues of the approaching conflict. There were several considerations which determined him to take this course. He believed, and not without reason, that very few volunteers could be obtained unless he would become one himself, and lead the way. Patriotism prompted the personal consecration. Then he felt that the young men of his congregation would be exposed to many temptations, and he wished to do what he could to preserve them from the vices so prevalent in the army. He acted from a solemn conviction of duty, and never had reason to regret the part he performed. The company went to Lancaster, and thence to Harrisburg.

Shortly before the organization of the regiment, a spirit of defection manifested itself in the company from Waynesburg. Some wished to return home; others murmured against the government regulations, and the majority, (there were honorable exceptions,) were contemplating a refusal to take the usual oath of fidelity. This becoming known to Mr. Thom, he was filled with anxiety. He felt that every available man was needed in those perilous times. The honor of his townsmen was at stake, and the existence of the regiment depended in no small extent upon the faithfulness of "Company C." He determined to prevent, if possible, a meeting proposed by the disaffected. Accordingly he assembled the company, as usual, for morning prayers and roll-call; after which he requested the men to remain a moment, intimating that he had a word to say to them. He then told them what he had heard, and what grief it had occasioned him. He spoke of the condition of the country, the peril of their homes, and the disgrace of passive submission to invasion. His address, which is reported to have been "very eloquent and soul-stirring," concluded with the declaration: "As for myself, I would rather die like a dog, than live a coward." The effect was all he desired. All complaints were hushed, and every man solemnly pledged himself to help drive the enemy beyond the Potomac.

. When arrived at Harrisburg, thêre was but little delay in organizing the regiment, the 47th P. V. M., and Mr. Thom was appointed Chaplain. From Harrisburg he wrote to his wife: "I got here safely last night about dark, I was not sick coming up, as I feared I would be, but feel very well to-day. O! how good God has been to me. I am sure I love Him. I have never felt so sure of it as I have done during these days, which otherwise were days of great affliction and distress. I am now in the way of being well cared for. I am much refreshed. I need not say my eyes are dim, and my heart yet feels the pressure of yours in our sad good-bye. I have felt very heavy and full of tears ever since. But I hope God will make us all the happier for our sufferings. God bless you, my dearest. *I* cannot bless you as I would. Tell Bertie to be a good boy and pray for papa. Tell Willie I think of him, and pray for him every day, and don't let him forget me. O! how his joyous 'papa, papa,' rings in my ears. . . . . Write to Harrisburg, 47th Pegiment P. M., care of Col. Wickersham. . . . . Now may you lean on our Beloved. Yours, J. C. THOM."

The regiment left Harrisburg as soon as its organization was completed, and marched to the Potomac just in time to see the Confederate army cross into Virginia. It remained encamped for several weeks, doing picket and guard duty, and was then ordered to Schuylkill county, to assist in keeping the miners quiet, and after a short time of service there, was mustered out in Reading, the latter part of August.

In this connection we will introduce a few extracts from letters addressed to Mrs. Thom.

"July 4, 1863. I am in such a state of excitement, that I can scarcely trust myself to write. We are in fearful suspense in regard to the battle now raging. I am completely unmanned. I have been weeping like a child, and am now choking back the tears with the utmost effort. But I can keep them away *now.* The marks on this page are the tears of heaven over the bloody field. I am in the big tent of the Christian Commission, and it is not proof against such a rain as this. You will know the truth before this reaches you, but the rumors are most painful, and the men are sent forward with a despatch that shows there is dreadful urgency. God make us another Independence day of this! . . . . Last night there was preaching in the tent, and I was enjoying the sermon very much, when a violent rain came on, and a terrific peal of thunder shook the earth. In a moment more Reese H—— came in, and rushing up to me, said one of our men was struck. I hastened away, and ordered the poor fellow to be drawn out into the pouring rain until a surgeon could be obtained. But life was gone. His name is Erb, came from near Lancaster, is the son of a wealthy German farmer. I attended to the poor boy, walked through the flooded camp, waded through ditches, got clean clothing, washed him with my own hands, dressed him, and laid him out as well as I could, and then at midnight laid down in my wet clothes on the ground, and slept till morning..... I am very well. I don't even feel tired. I dried myself at the camp-fire, and am quite comfortable. Tell Mr. Buchanan to send down for Mr. Reed, to preach some Sabbath, soon. I cannot tell you how kind he was to me. I am glad to hear that the hearts of our people are stirred up. I hope my absence will do more good, through God's grace, than my presence. ..... God bless you, my dear wife. Go to Jesus with all your troubles. Kiss my sweet boys."

At a later date, he writes of his religious enjoyment: "I have been greatly refreshed. We have delightful meetings here, in the big tent; precious gatherings around the throne of grace at our camp, and sweet communings in the tent. There are rebel prisoners here all the time. I talk to them often, and give them tracts. . . . Now, dearest, you will no doubt be too busy all the day to think much, but at night don't weep. Think of our blessed Lord, who is the bond between christians. Kiss our dear babes. God bless you, my sweet wife."

The whole term of military service was not long, but it was very hard on the men. They had to make long marches without the needed facilities for transportation. Their rations were poor, and distributed irregularly. Not being accustomed to such exposure, quite a number of them were attacked with fever and other diseases. Some twenty or thirty were lying sick at one time in an old mill near Hagerstown, which was used as a hospital.

The Chaplain of the regiment was a favorite from the first. He not only performed the duties of chaplain, but also those of postmaster, nurse, comforter, adviser, and keeper of the peace. He frequently walked long distances to get the regimental mails. No mother could wait more tenderly on a child, than he did on the sick, in the old mill. He went among the citizens of Hagerstown, and procured delicacies for the sick soldiers. He interested some benevolent ladies in their behalf, who visited them, and brought them medicines, and suitable articles of food. And when the regiment was ordered away, he remained behind until he saw those who were too ill to accompany it, properly cared for. As if by instinct, he seemed to find out wherever there was despondency, fault-finding, or ill-feeling, among the soldiers, and under his treatment the usual evils of camp life seemed to disappear. Says Colonel Wickersham, to whom the writer is indebted for much of the foregoing information: "There are those I know, who can date the beginning of their christian life from a talk with our chaplain in front of a tent, or around a camp-fire. Mr. Thom's discourses in the army were short, pointed, practical, and well suited to the circumstances of those to whom he spoke. His preaching was not only popular with the soldiers of his own regiment, but also with those of other regiments encamped in its vicinity, who frequently came to hear him, and the services were often attended by citizens, both ladies and gentlemen. On one Sabbath afternoon in particular, a hundred, or more people, came out to camp from Hagerstown, to attend our religious services, the ladies bringing tea and toast in one hand for those who were sick, and carrying hymn-books and Bibles in the other. I am free to say, that in all my experience, I never met a man so wholly unselfish, so perfectly willing to make sacrifices for the good of others. Toward myself he ever exhibited all the kindness of an affectionate brother."

The statements made by his friend, the colonel of the regiment, were fully confirmed by the officers and soldiers generally. Every one loved the chaplain. His influence seemed almost like magic. A word, a look, a visit, or a gift from him, seemed to win the soldier's heart at once. The love he received was merited, for he counted no toil or pain too great, if he could relieve the sick, or comfort and encourage the desponding. By kind attentions, and an example of consistent goodness, he made new friends every day. He was not only highly estemeed by his own regiment, but he secured the good-will and admiration of nearly all in the Brigade, for there were few that did not know the chaplain of the 47th. The most profane uttered no oaths in his presence, and confederate prisoners treated him with utmost respect. He sought the spiritual good of friend and foe, and his memory in the hearts of those who were converted by his ministry, or comforted by his loving words, is like the sweetest perfume, and shall never die. Colonel Wickersham, (for several years Principal of the State Normal School at Millersville, and more recently, State Superintendent of Common Schools in Pennsylvania,) became warmly attached to Mr. Thom. The affection was mutual, and these two friends spent at least a few pleasant hours together after "The cruel war was over." The Principal of the Waynesburg Academy, now Rev. E. W. Wherry, was with his pastor throughout this term of military service, and bears affectionate testimony to his faithfulness in all duty.

Another who was warmly attached to him, says, "I never shall forget one occasion of great interest, at the close of which, the men shouted, 'God bless our beloved chaplain,' and then rent the air with their thrice-repeated cheers."

When about to be mustered out of service, the company which he had been mainly instrumental in raising, gave him a large and beautiful photograph album, as a token of their appreciation of his singular kindness and fidelity.

CHAPTER XIII.

LAST DAYS AT WAYNESBURG.

AFTER his return from the army, he immediately resumed his work among his own people. His health was not good, but his labors were continued without intermission, until he was transferred to another charge. He preached with great faithfulness. There were sad evidences of spiritual declension. There had been much to divert the attention of the people from the great interests of religion. They had passed through troublous times, and some roots of bitterness had sprung up among them. Iniquity abounded, and the love of many had grown cold. He adapted his preaching to the condition of the church. He warned, exhorted, and entreated.

As the result of faithful labor, in public and private, there was a gradual improvement in the condition of the church generally, and in one part of his field there were special indications of the Spirit's presence. "At St. Marks," (formerly an Episcopalian Church,) said the pastor, "we have had many precious meetings, and Jesus was in the midst. His appeals to the unconverted were more than usually solemn. He seemed to have a presentiment that his work was nearly ended. With the earnestness of one who apprehended the awful wrath of God, he solemnly told his unconverted people of danger, and then besought them, with great affection, and earnest pleadings, to take refuge in Jesus from the gathering storm. There were several cases of hopeful conversion. He thanked God and took courage."

Several times during his ministry in Waynesburg, he had been invited to preach as a candidate before other churches which were considered, by those extending the invitations, as presenting wider fields of usefulness. He was called to the church in Columbia, Pennsylvania, and there were many considerations in favor of the change. But he did not feel satisfied that it was his duty to go, and the call was declined. He preached a Sabbath in Carlisle, Pennsylvania, after the resignation of Rev. W. W. Eells, and was strongly urged to suffer his name to be presented as a candidate for that charge, but he replied that he believed God still had a work for him in Waynesburg, and discouraged a call, which, if it had been formally made, he would have felt constrained to decline.

In May, 1865, he was invited to visit the Pine Street Church in St. Louis. This church, for several years, had been served with great acceptance by Rev. Dr. S. B. McPheeters. In consequence of troubles growing out of the condition of the country, Dr. McPheeters' pastoral relation to that people had been dissolved. Mr. Thom went to St. Louis in the month of July, and preached on three consecutive Sabbaths. His preaching made so favorable an impression on the people that a unanimous call to the pastorate of that church was extended to him soon after. Before he left the city, he was informed that a call would be given him, and he was asked to consider the subject of removal soon, in anticipation of formal action on the part of the church, as it was very desirable that the vacancy should be filled at an early period. His state of mind in reference to so important a question, may be gathered from letters written to his wife, near the close of his visit. "I don't want to come to St. Louis, unless my Heavenly Father says *come*, so clearly and imperatively that there can be no mistaking His will. May God direct us. ..... During my whole stay here, I have been enabled to draw nearer than usual to His throne, and to put more implicit trust in His wisdom and love. May He ever keep us near His side."

Again he writes: "The issues are with God. He has singularly managed and controlled this whole matter from its beginning. Let Him do with us as seemeth Him good, and blessed be His holy name."

After his arrival home the acceptance of this call was urged in several letters, written by members of the congregation. He was greatly perplexed for a time, and set apart a season of fasting and prayer for Divine direction. "I pray constantly, Lord, do with me as Thou wilt. Let me have no will but Thine. . . . . Lord, what wilt Thou have me to do." When at length persuaded that it was his duty to go to St. Louis, he at once addressed himself to the work of preparation for the removal. One consideration, which had much influence on his mind, was that of health. To one unacquainted with his peculiar physical condition, it might occur that the change, from a country to a city charge, would be unfavorable in this respect. But his experience at Natchez had been such as to encourage the hope that a warmer climate, and one more removed from the sea, would be highly advantageous. He had never been so well as in the south. The climate of eastern Pennsylvania, subject to sudden changes, and the atmosphere often ladened with saline moisture, had always been detrimental to his health. But the great question, and one, as he believed, clearly and affirmatively answered, was, "has the Lord a work for me to do in St. Louis?". Then I will leave all other interests in his hands.

He was warmly attached to the church in Waynesburg. It was his first charge. It was hard to sunder the ties, so strong and tender, which bound him to that people. He had thought to comfort the aged in their last years, and lay them to rest in the quiet church-yard. He had thought to stay long with his spiritual children, helping them by counsels and prayers, to stand fast in the Lord. He had thought, through many years, to care for the children of the church, on whose heads he had sprinkled the waters of baptism. True, there had been times of discouragement, when he felt it might be well for him to go elsewhere. But, like the magnetic needle, which disturbed for a little, soon returns to its rest, and points to the pole, so when the question of removal came, and occasioned anxious inquiries as to duty, it had been, before, only for a brief season, and his heart, clinging to his first love, refused to transfer its affections to others.

But now a voice says: "This is the way,

walk in it," and he must not disobey. Then there was a mingling of opposite emotions. To occupy so important a position as that to which he had been called; to labor for Christ in a centre of so great influence; to enjoy the varied advantages of residence in a pleasant city,—all these, and other considerations, made him thankful in the midst of sorrow.

One day he was conversing with a friend in reference to the proposed change. He was deeply sincere in his conviction that God was calling him to the west, and as he spake with much earnestness of St. Louis, the pride of the south-west, a controling centre in the valley of the Mississippi, drawing its commerce through great navigable rivers, and railroads extending to the Atlantic, and ere long to reach the Pacific, and alluded to the necessity of Christian effort in that growing city, which, through God's blessing, would be felt along the radiating lines of trade and travel, his friend felt that it was his duty to go, and hoped that he would become a tower of strength to our beloved church in that western city. But he adds: "I saw how great was the struggle, and how severe the suffering he endured, in separating himself from the people among whom he had labored so long. It was like tearing up by the roots a strong and vigorous oak which years of storm and sunshine had firmly set in its parent soil; with it must come much of the deep subsoil imbedded about and beneath its trunk."

His last sermons were very impressive, and the precious truths he uttered on those sad Sabbaths are treasured in many loving hearts. In a discourse on John xiv. 27, "Peace I leave with you, my peace I give unto you," &c., the following passages occur. "There is a pathetic interest attached to the parting of friends. When by long intercourse and mutual sympathy we are bound to each other by bonds of strong affection, there is a tenderness experienced in the hour of separation which makes every word thrill through the soul. I have looked through my tears into tear-dimmed eyes, and heard farewells that will ring in my ears until my dying day. . . . . This interest is increased and deepened when we feel that the parting is a final one. I have often pictured to myself the sad company that went with Paul a little way, when he started on his last journey to Jerusalem, sorrowing most of all at the words which he spake, that they should see his face no more. They were his companions in labor; the heroic women who, in spite of the terrors of the heathen mob, had ministered to his wants, and listened to his teachings; and there too were his spiritual children, as yet mere babes in the word, who needed instruction and care, and who entreated that they might be with him. How melting were their appeals when they prayed him not to go! How much more eloquent their silence, when Paul, struggling with his emotions, cried out: 'What mean ye, to weep, and break my heart!'"

Several weeks before he left Waynesburg there was an unusual amount of sickness among the people. Typhoid fever swept over the community. There were few families it did not enter, and in many households there was at least one vacant chair. There seemed a sickness in the very air. Deep awe settled down on almost every home. The people spoke in subdued tones, and a care-worn or anxious expression sat on every face. It was such a time as must be felt in order to be understood, and being felt, can never be forgotten. Such were his last days in Waynesburg. He was much among the sick and dying; and continually pressed with all the care and anxiety incident to removal from a much loved home. He had no time for general visiting, and as many of his people as were able to leave their homes called on him.

Great was the grief of the church. The sorrow was general. Very touching were the last interviews of pastor and people. Memory reverts to them with tears, and revives the sadness of the parting hours. In one house the sad farewell was spoken at the bed-side of a sick child. After the stricken household had joined their beloved minister in the last prayer he offered in their home-sanctuary, with an almost breaking heart, the mother said: "For all I am as a Christian, I am indebted, under God, to you." And then with deep emotion, spoke of her great unwillingness to have him go to another people.

In another family was a dying girl. The shadow of death was on her face when he stood beside her bed. She could not see him, but she knew his voice, and that tender touch who could mistake? She raised her thin white hand and laid it in his, saying: "My dear, pastor I do love you, and I love Jesus." This she repeated many times, and then, in faltering accents, invoked 'God's blessing on the head of the weeping servant of Christ. A little after, she went home to Jesus, and the Good Shepherd more than filled the pastor's place.

Further on was a sick child, cared for by strangers. There was an unnatural brilliancy in her eye, and her whole appearance was calculated to melt the heart in deepest piety. The child thanked him in saddest tones. He wept with her, and then gave her his last benediction.

There was another, a woman of peculiar cares, of a meek, quiet, and loving spirit, who walked a long distance to meet her pastor in his own home. Great was her grief to learn that he was absent, but she was assured he would not leave without calling on her. Late in the evening he went to see her. They wept together. She said, "I fear we will never meet again." He replied, "I hope we shall have many sweet meetings on earth, but, if God has ordered otherwise, let us prepare to meet in heaven. *There* are no sad partings."

Standing on another day, beside a grave, in which the remains of a dear youth had been deposited, the bereaved mother came to him, weeping, and said: "O! Mr. Thom, how can I part with you?" Then she pointed to the grave of her only daughter, and said: "I had to part with her, and must I give you up too?" He looked at her with unspeakable tenderness, took her hand in his, and said: "God bless you, Mrs. W——. Look upward." He could say no more. It was not long until through flowing tears she looked upward to that un-

20*

clouded land whither the spirit of her loved pastor had gone.

There was an aged Christian woman who lived in an humble cottage beyond the mountain, several miles away, whom he went to see late at night. This godly woman consecrated her son to Jesus, and to the work of missions, when a helpless babe he lay in the cradle. The offering was accepted. He gave himself to Jesus in early life, and went as a missionary to Africa. One day, when sailing near the coast, he was drowned. When the sad news reached the mother, she wept for a little, then dried her tears, as she thought of the sweet home above, and said: "Well, George is nearer to me in heaven, than he would have been in Africa." With a sad heart the pastor left this dear Christian woman. She was very feeble, and seemed to be quite near the grave. As he rode home, far on in the night, he said to the friend beside him: "I fear I shall never see that good mother in Israel again, till I meet her in the house not made with hands." Contrary to all probability she outlived him, and sent messages of sympathy to his widow, after he had gone home to God.

The last Sabbath came, and the last sermon was preached, with an open coffin before the pulpit. He told his people he could not preach a farewell discourse, but would address them in a simple gospel sermon, about One who is altogether lovely. He preached from the words: "I have loved thee with an everlasting love." (Jeremiah xxi. 3.) Near the close of his sermon, which was but partially written, he made this prophetic remark: "Perhaps on the distant shores of eternity, I shall be permitted to watch for your coming, and wait to welcome you, as one by one, you enter the eternal home." He made a few remarks to his spiritual children, closing with these words: "My little children, love one another, and may that everlasting love, which is all my desire and all my hope, be and abide with you all for ever." This was uttered in a tone so touching, that it will never be forgotten. His last utterance was: "O! my people, my heart's desire and prayer to God is, and long has been, that you might all be saved." Then followed the prayer, the solemn hymn, the last benediction, and his work in Waynesburg was ended.

His last hours were spent with his noble-hearted physician, whose steadfastness was manifested in the dark days that followed, and then, with his wife and boys, he turned away from the only home they were ever permitted to enjoy together. They knew it not, and it was well.

"We have had our May, my darling,
  And our roses long ago,
And the time of the year is coming, my dear,
  For the silent night and the snow!

"And God is God, my darling,
  Of night, as well as of day:
We feel and know that we can go,
  Wherever he leads the way.

"Ah, God of the night, my darling,
  Of the night of death so grim:
The gate that leads out of life, good wife,
  Is the gate that leads to Him."

CHAPTER XIV.

DEATH AT ST. LOUIS, MISSOURI.

LEAVING behind him the people for whom he had cared so kindly, and to whom he had preached so faithfully for *over seven* years; looking for the last time on the home where his boys had been born, where the love-light had never grown dim, but had increased with every trial, he hastened to his work in St. Louis, stopping only a short time at Bedford, and Blairsville, Pennsylvania, leaving his family at the latter place.

God has said, "Thou knowest not what a day may bring forth." We long to know what lies in the future, and think that if we could foresee the results of causes which we have set in operation, or the consequences of relations we propose to form, then we could advance with a calm, intelligent step, and bring to a desirable consummation the plans of life. But there are no available sources of information; no voice in the winds, no prophecy in the stars, no foreshadowing of events in the flight of birds, or the course of the tempest. Superstition has sought the heights and the depths for the coveted knowledge. History has thought to trace the future by borrowing light from the past. Philosophy tells of general laws and secondary causes; still the veil is unlifted, and the word of God is unchanged: "Ye know not what shall be on the morrow."

The best matured plan may issue in disappointment; the most endearing relation may terminate in an hour, and prospective good may disappear like the mists of the morning. The Christian religion teaches us that God directs our steps, and orders our lot. The Infinite Mind traces the pathway of the future, then spreads His cloud upon it. We must walk by faith, and not by sight.

Then, too, the dispensations of Providence are often mysterious. There is darkness behind, as well as before us. "Thy way is in the sea, and Thy path in the great waters, and Thy footsteps are not known." It was a sad day to many when Judson and Newell, with their wives, left their native country to labor among the heathen in a far-off land. With a strong conviction of duty, a calm trust in God, and the hope of great usefulness, these first missionaries went forth to their blessed work. A few months pass by, and the sad intelligence reaches this country that Harriet Newell is dead! On the Isle of France, almost in sight of her proposed field of labor, she awaits the morning of the resurrection. How dark the providence! Though in some respects peculiar, this case is a representative of a great multitude. The subject of the present Memoir is one of these. He had scarcely entered on his work in St. Louis when God met him, changed his countenance, and took him away.

He commenced his labors in the Pine Street Church, on the first Sabbath of October, 1865. After preaching three Sabbaths, he was suddenly recalled to Pennsylvania, by the dangerous illness of his eldest boy. The journey was one of great anxiety. He had but little expectation of seeing his child alive. Arrived at a railroad station near Blairsville, a friend met him with the pleasant intelligence that his little son was much better, and supposed to be out of danger. When he entered the sick chamber, his face was brightened with hope, and his first expression was one of gratitude, "My darling, God is good." His next thought was to secure rest for his wife, by taking upon himself the almost exclusive care of the child. On Sabbath morning he preached for the Rev. Mr. Hill, in the Presbyterian Church. When urged to preach again, at night, his wife remonstrated, on the ground that he needed rest. He replied, with that tenderness of manner which marked his last days, even beyond his habit: "My dear, I feel that I cannot lose this opportunity of speaking for Jesus."

During the two weeks that he sat at the bedside of his suffering boy, the fresh baptism of the Holy Spirit, which had evidently descended upon him, was such as to fill the mind of his wife with an indefinable dread. She could not analyze her feelings, but she experienced an exceeding longing to be in St. Louis, with all her dear ones around her, and no separation in prospect. A great sorrow was casting its shadow before.

As soon as it was practicable to leave his family, Mr. Thom returned to St. Louis. He left Pittsburg on Thursday night, October 26th, hoping to reach the end of his journey on Saturday. But detentions on the way delayed his arrival until Sabbath morning. Though very weary, and suffering from the unusual exposures of the journey, he prepared himself for the Sabbath services, and preached both morning and evening. It was observed by many that his health was much impaired. The causes for this were obvious. But, though very unwell, he preached two consecutive Sabbaths, lectured on Wednesday evenings, conducted the usual prayer-meeting on Friday evening, and commenced pastoral visitations. On the second Sabbath, his physician, Dr. Marshall, who was also one of the elders of the church, noticing that he was greatly indisposed, urged him to omit the night service. He replied, "I will wait until evening, and see how I feel." He went home with his friend, Mr. Ferguson, and rested during the remainder of the day. He was again urged to desist from preaching, but a sense of duty constrained him to make the attempt. He selected for his text, Matt. xxi. 28. Instead of entering the pulpit, he stood on the platform in front of it. He preached with great earnestness and power, and, as he subsequently remarked to Rev. Mr. Niccolls, "with great joy to his own soul." Before pronouncing the benediction, he rose and said: "the rapid throbbings of my pulse admonish me to say one word more." Then he urged his hearers, with great solemnity, to to accept Christ and His great salvation. The scene was strangely impressive. Many thought it ominous of an event which soon followed. His work was done. His last public appeal to sinners was spoken, and he left the Pine Street Church never to enter it again—alive.

He went that evening to the house of a kind

Christian lady, (Mrs. Fenby) where he remained until, after a painful illness of three weeks, his spirit went home to heaven. In the family alluded to, he received every attention he needed. Drs. Marshall, and Johnson; the elders of the church, and the ministers of the city, did all they could to alleviate his sufferings, and comfort him in his affliction. Several ladies ministered to him with affectionate sympathy, and unwearied patience. Stricken and grateful hearts cherish the memory of those kind attentions, and invoke heavenly benisons on the heads of those who gave them. The Master says, "I was sick, and ye visited *me.*" And the female servant who cared so faithfully for the dying man, and mourned so bitterly for him when dead, is not forgotten, either here or in heaven. The lowly Saviour, Christ in all, give her a place in the kingdom of His glory!

During the early part of his sickness, Mr. Thom was much concerned for his family. They were then with Mrs. Thom's brother, Dr. W. C. Bracken, in Ohio. He was frequently heard to say, "What will become of my poor wife!" A dear friend who came every day and arranged his bed, because he fancied it was more comfortable when she made it, urged him to send for Mrs. Thom. But with his usual self-forgetfulness, he said he could not think of asking her, when so worn with the care of sick children, to undertake the journey. At length, however, he consented. He wished the news of his sickness to be conveyed to her in a manner that would not excite unnecessary alarm. He also requested a telegram to be sent to Rev. Mr. Nixon, in Indianapolis, asking him to assist her in making the change of cars at that city. Subsequently, in his delirium, he was greatly distressed, supposing some great evil had befallen her. She came with her little boys, immediately after she was apprised of his condition. The eldest child was then convalescent, but the younger brother was dangerously ill when they arrived in St. Louis. Mrs. Thom was quite unprepared to find her husband so much reduced. When she entered the sick room, the wonted smile and warm welcome were wanting. There was an expression of intense suffering in his face. He extended his tremulous arms, and embraced, first, his wife, and then his darling boys. It was several moments before he spoke, and then he said to his wife: "This is a sad, sweet meeting, dear. I have suffered greatly, but I am better now." He then made some inquiries about the journey, and she replied briefly. Then looking at her very earnestly, he said, "You are a brave woman." After a little, he insisted that she should go to another room and rest, which, to gratify him, and yet very reluctantly, she did.

In the afternoon of the same day he said, "I begin to indulge the hope that I shall live and not die, that I may declare the glory of God. For a while I thought my recovery doubtful." Two days later, on Saturday, Mrs. Thom, who was watching her sick boy in an adjoining room, thought he called her. She hastened to his bed and asked him what he wished. He said he had not called her. "I was just asking God to make me well." With all the cheerfulness she could command, she said, "Will He not do it?" He replied, sadly, "I don't know."

A great deal of the time he was engaged in prayer, and often spoke of the goodness of God, and the preciousness of Christ. Conversing with a friend, he referred to his ministry, and said: "It seems to me that I have new views of the Saviour, and that if I am spared, I can preach as I never before have done." His thoughts were often with the church. He was anxious that the pulpit should be supplied, and suggested plans for promoting the growth, and increasing the efficiency of the church. Often in his delirium, fancying he was in the pulpit, he would rise from his pillow and entreat those who were near him to love Jesus. Then he would follow his pathetic appeals with prayer, and on one occasion, announced the hymn beginning,

> "God moves in a mysterious way
> His wonders to perform."

At another time he extended his trembling hands and said, in thrilling accents, that moved all to tears, "My heart's desire and prayer to God for you all, is that you may be saved"— his parting words to the church at Waynesburg.

One day, when Mrs. Thom entered his room, he said, "I have had refreshing sleep." She did not fully catch his remark, and supposing he had spoken of receiving grateful food from some friend, asked who had sent it. He replied, "God, for so He giveth His beloved sleep." At night he called Mr. Niccolls, who, at his request, had lain down in an adjoining room; "Come to me, for I am passing through deep waters." Mr. Niccolls talked with him, directed his attention to the Lamb of God, and then prayed for him. Presently he was comforted, and said, "Now, go and lie down again, for I am not alone." After this, his friend tells us, "No doubt clouded his mind, no fear disturbed the joyful repose of his soul. His faith seemed to lift him up into the Divine presence, and he saw everything from that great centre of the soul's life—Jesus Christ. This was manifested even in the delirium produced by his disease. As on some wrecked ship, whose timbers are parting to the blows of the waves, the compass still points true to the north, undisturbed by the ruin around, so his faith, while all else was wild and disordered at the approach of death, looked forth clearly and unfailingly to Him who has conquered death."

For several days he was very much distressed for his sick child, often ejaculating, "My poor boy!"—"My poor boy!" When he was told that the physicians entertained no hope of his child's recovery, he seemed, for a moment, to be pleased with the thought of having his boy go with him to heaven. He made an effort to speak, but was only heard to say, "Arms—tender—Shepherd." Then he turned to his wife, with a look of unutterable pity, which it almost seemed must bear her away with him, and said: "But I am so sorry for you." Presently his eldest son was brought to his bedside. "This," said Mrs. Thom, "is your first-born, the son of your love. What is your message to him?" All the unbounded affection of the father beamed from his face as he looked upon his boy. He kissed him, and then said: "Bertie, put your hands on my face." Then turning to the mother, added: "Tell him always to love Jesus."

One evening the elders, who were watching with him, adjusted his pillow, and he seemed to recognize them. He said, in a distinct voice: "Now I will give you my blessing," and then pronounced upon them such a benediction as can only come from the borders of the unseen world.

On Sabbath morning, the 26th of November, his symptoms became more alarming. Then, for the first time, his wife realized his danger, but forced back the wail of agony into her breaking heart, and shut it there. Kind friends said they would watch with the sick child, for now it mattered not who ministered to him, as he recognized no one. The hours of Sabbath night crept on, and the life of the minister was waning. "I have no hope," said Mr. Niccolls, "but in the prayer of faith." When the morning came, "No hope," was written on every face. During an interval of consciousness, he endeavored to speak to his wife. Mr. Niccolls caught the words and repeated them. "He is telling you how much he has loved you; how much he loves you now; how happy you have always made him." Then, with a rapturous look, and in clear, loud tones, which all could hear, Mr. Thom added: "But O! to see Jesus—to see Jesus!—O! the joy of seeing Jesus!"

At another time he turned to his wife with a look of inexpressible affection, which startled all in the room. It seemed as if the love of a whole lifetime was concentrated in that one look. He then commended her to Jesus, the ever-living and all-sufficient Friend.

On Monday morning his breathing became very difficult, and continued so. Not long before he died, Mr. Niccolls asked him if he knew his wife, who stood at his bed-side; but he made no reply. When asked again who was speaking to him, he could not tell. But when asked, still further, if he knew Christ, he replied with a smile: "O, yes, He is all my salvation, and all my joy." Shortly after, he uttered aloud an earnest prayer for the church. About midnight Mr. Niccolls again asked him if he knew his wife. He replied, "I do know my sweet wife. Where is she?" She bent over him, and he endeavored to raise his arms, but he could not do it unaided. Mr. Niccolls and Mr. Ferguson assisted him, and he took his wife's face between his hands and tried to speak. Only one word was heard—"heaven." He never spoke again. A little while after Mr. N. said: "Mr. Thom, if you are still trusting in Jesus, raise your hand." His gesture told that he was still clinging to the precious Lamb of God. The morning came, and his spirit passed so quietly, and so sweetly away, that the little group in the death-chamber, scarcely knew when it was gone. Presently some one remarked: "He is dead." Just then a bright angel opened the gate of heaven, and said: "Alive forevermore." It was the morning of Tuesday, Nov. 28, 1865. Mr. Niccolls offered a very touching prayer, giving back the soul to God, thanking Him for a life so beautiful and so useful, and the widow calmly closed the eyes which had never looked upon her but in purest love. He died in the 36th year of his age.

The funeral services were held in the Pine Street Church on the Thursday following. The remains of the departed servant of God were placed in front of the pulpit, the place from which he had spoken his last words as an ambassador of Christ. The coffin was wreathed with flowers entwined by the hands of affection. The sermon was preached by Rev. Samuel J. Niccolls, the warm and steadfast friend of the deceased. The Rev. Thomas A. Bracken, of Lebanon, Kentucky, (Mrs. Thom's brother,) and Miss Lavinia Thom, (the sister of the departed minister,) were the only relatives who witnessed the sad solemnities of that funeral day. Rev. Drs. Brooks, and Anderson, with Reverends McCook, Mutchmore, and others, participated in the services. The remains were then conveyed to the Bellefontaine Cemetery, and were interred in a pleasant spot, dedicated for the purpose by Mr.

Whitehill, a venerable and beloved elder of the Pine Street Church. The bereaved congregation erected a suitable monument over the grave, on which was engraven the name and age of the deceased, and the simple inscription,

SAVED BY GRACE:

the theme of his ministry on earth, and the burden of his song in heaven.

SERMON

ON

THE RESURRECTION.

BY THE

REV. JOHN C. THOM.

The following sermon is introduced as an appropriate conclusion to the Memoir of the author. Though less carefully prepared than many of his discourses were, yet it will give the reader a very correct idea of his style of sermonizing, and, at the same time, the precious truth it unfolds may comfort some sorrowing ones, by leading their thoughts onward to the glad morning of the resurrection.

SERMON.

Acts xxvi. 8.

WHY SHOULD IT BE THOUGHT A THING INCREDIBLE WITH YOU, THAT GOD SHOULD RAISE THE DEAD?

THERE are two books on which the writing of God's finger is seen; the books of Nature and Revelation: and these never disagree—one may contain a lesson not found in the other, and so they may be supplementary, but they can never be contradictory—the rotation of the earth, and its revolution around the sun, could never have been learned from the Bible, for they are truths which do not come within the range of its teachings. But the Bible, when properly understood, supports no opposing theory. So also, nature itself could never have taught the fact of an atonement, though it most strongly hints at its necessity. This agreement, of course, results from their common authorship. God cannot contradict himself. But it is also the foundation of an important principle to us. We are never required to believe anything which is abhorrent to the unbiassed judgment. Those laws and regulations which God has written upon our souls are never violated or set at defiance by the laws He has given in the inspired volume. A careful distinction must, however, always be made between what is contradictory to reason, and what is higher than reason,—even between what is improbable, and what is incredible. One, reasoning beforehand, might say there was a strong antecedent improbability that Christ would leave the throne of His glory, and come to this world, to be a servant, obedient even unto death, for us. And yet when we remember He is a God of infinite goodness and love, it is not incredible. I can believe it. It is higher than my unaided reason could soar. My reason reaches scarcely beyond the idea of a man laying down his life for his friend. But here is the Son of God dying, while we are yet enemies. But it does not contradict my reason, for reason itself teaches that the ways of God are higher than those of man. But when I am asked to believe that sprinkling water on a man, without any agency of his own, has completely changed his whole nature, though I see him act and feel just as wickedly as before; or, that by a few words of a priest, a piece of bread has been changed into the body, and soul, and divinity of Christ, though I see, and feel, and taste it still to be bread, just as it was before, it is contradictory to reason, and I must refuse my credence.

It is true that many things are pronounced to be incredible by the advocates of a one-sided philosophy, which are clearly reasonable, as for example, that the sins of a finite creation should be punished with suffering in this life, and with endless misery in the life to come. But a clearly revealed truth cannot be set aside upon such *ex parte* judgment. The incendiary, doubtless, thinks it unreasonable that the act of a moment should be punished with ten years of hard labor; yet the judge does not hesitate in his sentence, and he is fully borne out by the judgment of an enlightened community. The Apostle recognizes this great principle in his defence before Festus and Agrippa, and bases all his claims to be heard, upon the credibility of the doctrine he was ready to die to defend—"why should it be thought a thing incredible with you, that God should raise the dead?" If it be incredible, I claim no hearing, but if it be not contradictory to reason, I have such strong assurance of its truth, that I, like the saints of old, am ready to be tortured, not accepting deliverance, in hope of a better resurrection, and would to God that you all were altogether such as I am, except these bonds. My object, to-day, is to establish the credibility of the doctrine of the resurrection, and its consequent claims upon our belief.

By resurrection, we do not mean that spiritual restoration, which is sometimes called by that name; for Paul taught that both the just and the unjust should be raised from the dead. Nor do we mean simply the appearance, and existence of the soul, in a future world;

for as we hold that the soul never loses its consciousness—is never dead—it cannot properly be said to be raised. But we mean the resuscitation and resurrection of the body, to be united again with the disembodied spirit, to enjoy or suffer the just recompense of the deeds done on the earth. The very first ground of credibility is implied in the text. It is a work of God. It is not claimed that these bodies, which seem so subject to disease, decay, and death, contain an inherent power of reconstruction; that after their long sleep in the dust they shall, of themselves, come, atom to atom, and bone to bone, shake off the slumber of the grave, and arise. That would indeed be incredible. But the case is altogether different when it is declared that all this is accomplished by the power of God. It is not incredible, because God clearly has power sufficient to accomplish it. He who gathered our dust at the beginning, and formed all this strange machinery of nerves and muscles, bones and sinews, veins and arteries, and then caused the lungs to breathe, the heart to beat, and the vital current to flow, without a moment's intermission, all through these years; He is able to reconstruct and reanimate the fabric, after he has allowed it to fall to decay. We know that nothing short of Divine power can accomplish it. God's eye follows every human being through all the streets and lanes of life; and let them make the pillow for their last sleep in the wilds of the unbroken forest, in the dens and caves of the earth,—amid the coral reefs, and unknown habitations of the deep blue sea;—or let them send forth the spirit amid the roar and crackling of devouring fire, and know when they all are

> "Flung to the heedless winds
> And scattered to the blast,
> Their ashes can be watched,
> And gathered at the last,"

and earth and sea, and death and hell, be compelled to give up their dead. But it may be urged, though God be clearly able to raise the body, there is no sufficient reason why he should do so. There are many things which God is able to do, which we cannot believe he would do without sufficient motive. For example, God can cast all the angels out of heaven, or destroy all men from the earth, but we cannot believe he will do so, without any reason. So, if any attribute of the Divine nature is violated by it, we cannot believe that God will raise the dead.

I remark again, therefore, that it is not incredible, because it is in accordance with the *wisdom* of God. God does all his works for the highest possible ends. To say that anything could have a higher or better object than it has, would be to call in question the wisdom and goodness of the Creator. Now, does it accord with those ideas which God has given us of wisdom, that such a strange, compound being, should be called from the dust of the earth, and clothed with the image of his Creator, to spend his life like a tale that is told, and then lie down in the grave and be seen no more? "What a piece of work is a man! How noble in reason! how infinite in faculties! in form and moving how express and admirable! in action, how like an angel! in apprehension, how like a God! the beauty of the world! the paragon of animals!" shall this noble structure fall so soon into irretrievable decay? Shall this temple endure but threescore years and ten, and then be cast down, and not one stone be left upon another? Shall this human face divine, the mirror of a thousand varied thoughts, be darkened by an eternal night? Shall this human frame become the cadaverous corpse, the reeking feast of corruption and the worm, the naked skeleton, the silent dust, and then nothing? Why, if this be all, the structures of men have outlived a hundred generations. Shall the pyramids, erected like ant-hills, by the toil of myriads of men, outlast, for untold ages, their God-built builders? As far as we are informed, man is an order of beings unknown elsewhere in the universe—a compound of body and spirit, midway between earth and heaven. Now, in the beautiful variety of God's creation, shall the important link be wanting? Shall man, as such, be blotted out of existence, his spirit go into the ranks of the angels, and his body fall into unformed and shapeless matter? or shall this noble structure be rebuilt, this corruptible put on incorruption, and this mortal put on immortality, and ten thousand thousand redeemed souls, not unclothed, but clothed upon with glorious bodies, stand in the armies of heaven, and shout God's praises for ever and ever? Why should it be thought a thing incredible with you, that God should raise the dead?

It is also agreeable to the justice of God. Not only does the soul transgress the law of God, but the body is also an instrument of sin. Not only is the spirit of God's children obedient to his commands; they serve him with their bodies and spirits, which are the Lord's. Now, is it not reasonable that the body shall be partaker of suffering or enjoyment in the world to come? In this world the body, as well as the soul, endures the consequences of sin. While the soul languishes and mourns, the body, also, is broken and decrepit. Shall this even-handed justice cease in the future ordinances of God? When Cranmer came to the stake, he thought his remorse and penitence of soul were not, alone, sufficient punishment for his sin, but he thrust his right-hand, which had signed his recantation, into the scorching fire till it was consumed. Shall not the right hand of forgery, of rapine, and murder, the tongue of deceit, and the body of voluptuousness and debauchery, suffer with the soul which they served as the instruments of iniquity? As the whole man, body and soul, is the criminal here, shall not the whole man, body and soul, suffer the penalty? We know not what that penalty may be, and we have no right to speculate. We know it will be unspeakably dreadful, and we have no right to expect that any part of our being, body or soul, will escape the vengeance of an outraged Deity. It is reasonable, on account of his justice, that God should raise the dead.

Still further, the *mercy* of God is interested in the resurrection of man. We enjoy many pleasures in this world. Some of them are high and holy. But are these all which the boundless love of our Father in heaven has prepared for those who love him? Are these the joys which eye hath not seen, nor ear heard, nor mind conceived? Nay, boundless goodness must have a wider range, a higher height, and a deeper depth. But it may be said, these future enjoyments belong to the soul alone. In the first place, that supposes man to be a totally different being, in the world to come; for all the enjoyments we have in our souls in this world, come directly, or indirectly, through the bodily senses. We learn even the word of God, the way of salvation, through the eyes and ears of the fleshly body, and we pray and praise with our lips of clay. It is a popular idea that these dull clods impede the action of the spirit, and we would be better off without them. It is true that this body is corrupted and defaced by sin. But it is a glorious body still. It was built at first by the hand of God himself, for high and holy purposes, and wrecked as it is, it is still the instrument, and, as far as we can see, almost the only instrument, through which impressions are made upon the soul, or through which the soul acts upon the world without; and so, then, instead of being better off without the body, if stripped of it, we would lose the great means of our power and enjoyment. The spirits of the just will be happy in their disembodied state, but they will not be perfect till reunited, and both soul and body are glorified together. And even were this not so, shall the bodies of the children of God be deprived in heaven of all those enjoyments which they experience here? Shall the thrill of health and vigor be felt no more? Shall the soft breath of the evening breeze never kiss the immortal cheek? Shall the hand no more feel the grasp of pure affection, when in the great assembly we stand in high raptures around the throne of our glorified Redeemer? When contemplating the prison-house of Eternal Justice we shrink back, overawed by the dread secrecy of God, but when he has clearly revealed that the treasure of his everlasting love will be opened to the redeemed from among men, is it incredible that the body should be raised, that the whole man, body and soul, should rejoice together?

As I have shown that the resurrection is not incredible as an act of God's power, and demanded by his attributes, so I might also show it is not opposed to the feelings and instincts God has given to man. Why do we adorn the graves of friends? Why, like Mary, do we go and weep there? Why do we shrink back, often in spite of all our philosophy, from being torn to pieces after our death, or from lying in an unknown grave? Why do we rejoice to think our couch will be strewed with flowers, and watered with tears? It is because God has taught us that even our dead bodies are sacred, are held in reserve for a future life, and we cannot unteach ourselves, try as we may. Why is it, when we think of heaven, we think of the redeemed as well as of the Redeemer, and expect to see them there? I had a dear young friend in our neighboring city. She died of a lingering disease. It was a glorious sight to see that pure young saint putting off, day by day, the earthly house, and growing more and more like heaven. She had given her short life to the service of her Saviour, and now that she felt his hand leading her gently down into the cold river, there was no starting back, no fear: it was the unshrinking step of the child which feels its father's arms around it. But as she grew weaker, and the gate of heaven seemed to be nearer, and she saw the multitude which no man can number, around the throne of God, one thought oppressed her: might not her mother be separated from her side, and be lost to her among so many? After telling her mother her misgiving, she said, "Mother, when you die, be buried by my side, and when Jesus comes, we will rise together. I will take your hand, and together we will go to glory, and I will never, never let you go." Call it not a childish fancy. Call it not superstition. There is something in every good man's heart, which responds to such a feeling. It is God saying to us, that "these dead bodies shall arise again." "Awake and sing, ye that dwell in the dust, for thy dew is as the dew of herbs, and the earth shall cast out her dead." I might also add, there are a thousand analogies in nature which seem strongly to hint at a resurrection. But the truth seems so strong, and clear, and glorious, I have no heart for any more analogies. You have often heard them presented. The crawling worm, which seems to be lifeless for a while, bursts its cerements, and comes forth in a form of beauty, and floats away upon golden wings. The tree, stripped of its foliage, stands bare, and apparently lifeless, amid the storms of winter, but it buds and blooms in the spring. The seed, cast into its grave, springs up, and brings forth much fruit. Even the little brook which goes sparkling through your green fields, is consumed away by the drought of summer, but it is not lost. It goes to the clouds of heaven, and returns again upon the earth. Of all these you have heard, and they teach us that it is not a thing incredible that God should raise the dead.

It is true, that God's power is clearly sufficient to raise the dead. It is true, that God's wisdom, and justice, and goodness, seem to demand the resurrection. It is true, that man's instincts and desires, given him by his Maker, point to a resurrection. It is true, there are ten thousand analogies in nature, which indicate a resurrection. All this is true; but all this is not enough, when hell rolls beneath us; "for if the dead rise not, then is not Christ raised; and if Christ be not raised, your faith is vain, ye are yet in your sins; and they also which are fallen asleep in Christ are perished." God has not, therefore, left us with an uncertain light. He has cast the full blaze of his word upon this momentous subject, so that he that runs may read. Here the strife is ended, our doubts are set at rest, and life and immortality clearly brought to light. It is difficult to select proofs from the Bible, when the whole volume takes a resurrection for granted. Job, one of the most ancient of the worthies, triumphed over all his temptations and sufferings by this reflection: whatever might befall him here, even though he should be crushed to the grave, and devoured by corruption, he should sleep in the dust but a little while. Stand back, ye enemies! The day of your triumph will soon be over. "I know that my Redeemer liveth, and that he shall stand at the latter day upon the earth; and though after my skin worms destroy this body, yet in my flesh shall I see God; whom I shall see for myself, and mine eyes shall behold, and not another, though my reins be consumed within me." David's view was no less clear. Even when the wicked oppressed him, and his deadly enemies compassed him about, he says, "My heart is glad, and my glory rejoiceth; my flesh also shall rest in hope." "As for me, I will behold thy face in righteousness: I shall be satisfied, when I awake with thy likeness." Isaiah saw God roll back the covering cast over all people, and swallow up death in victory. Ezekiel saw the great multitude of dead, separated and scattered upon the earth, and yet at the breath of God's Spirit, they came, bone to his bone, and the dead arose and lived, an exceeding great army. Daniel says, "Many of them that sleep in the dust of the earth shall awake, some to everlasting life, and some to shame and everlasting contempt." Hosea saw the prison of the grave invaded, and the power of death broken; he heard God's voice: "I will ransom them from the power of the grave; I will redeem them from death; O death, I will be thy plagues! O grave, I will be thy destruction!" Paul himself applies this language to the resurrection, and as he kindles at the glorious prospect, he bursts out, "O death, where is thy sting? O grave, where is thy victory?" When we come to the New Testament, the subject is even more clearly brought out. God is declared to be the God of those who went into the grave two thousand years before, yet he is not the God of the dead, but of the living. Abraham, Isaac, and Jacob were not dead, they were but sleeping. "Marvel not at this," says Christ, "for the hour is coming in the which all that are in the grave shall hear his voice, and shall come forth." "I am the resurrection and the life." Nay, the scene itself is described. Christ, as Judge and

King, is seated upon the throne. The trumpet sounds. The dead awake. They shake off the clods of the grave, and come forth. The holy angels gather the vast assembly around the throne, and they stand, according to their merit, at the right hand and the left.

The apostles, we are told again and again, preached Jesus, and the resurrection of the dead. Paul professedly discusses the subject in an entire chapter, the xv. of 1 Corinthians. And John, after he had pointed forward to it, through the whole of the Apocalypse, when he came toward the close, and was about to finish the Book of inspiration, and seal it for ever, leaves these words ringing upon our ears, among the last of inspired utterances. He, the last survivor, looks back over the blood-stained graves of all the apostles, and multitudes of the saints of the Lord, who had been crucified, and burnt, and stoned, and sawn asunder, and then he glanced forward to their reward. "I saw," says he, "the dead, small and great, stand before God; and the books were opened; and the dead were judged out of those things which were written in the books, according to their works. And the sea gave up the dead which were in it; and death and hell delivered up the dead which were in them."

Do we need more assurance? Is it still a vague and uncertain thing? Christ, in pity for our weakness, has done even more. He has shown his power over death. He called the sleeping, and they awoke; and he himself, when he was bound with the chains of death, and sealed up in the grave, conquered the conqueror upon his throne. He rose, he burst the bands of death, and triumphed over the grave! Now, since our glorious Head has ascended upon high, we also shall be raised up. These were the considerations which filled the mind of Paul, when he stood so fearlessly, chained as he was, in the presence of Festus and Agrippa. What to him were the chain, and the dungeon, and the rack, and the cross itself, when he knew that his bruised, and lashed, and scarred body, would be raised a glorious body, and every mark of the conflict would be a badge of honor? What to him was the august presence of governors and kings, when he knew he should stand in the presence of the hosts of heaven, and the Judge of the quick and dead? None of these things moved him, neither did he count his life dear to himself, so that he might finish his course with joy.

My dear friends, does this glorious truth seem a reality to you? Is the grave a place of rest, and death, and sleep, and are all the interests of this short life clustered around the time of waking? Then what matters the toils and troubles of to-day? What matters it, if we be poor and despised? When we awake, and come forth to glory, and honor, and eternal life, these griefs shall all be forgotten. Let me be a sufferer, let me be a beggar, let me be a slave in this short hour of my existence, if I may thus obtain a better resurrection. But you that live at ease, and lay up no treasure against the time to come, what a miserable awaking will that be? How you will cling to your coffins, and hug the walls of the grave! How you will hide your head in the dust, and long to cover yourself again with corruption, but in vain! No marble monument, no towering pyramid, no, not the Alps or Andes, heaped upon your breast, can hold you in your tomb. You, too, shall hear the voice of God and live. Oh, turn now! Fly to the Saviour! Give him your service. Fight the good fight. Bespeak your crown, and your throne. Then shall your heart be glad, and your glory rejoice. Your flesh, also, shall rest in hope. Then shall you also be satisfied when you awake, not in this decrepit, diseased, and dying form, but in the glorious likeness of the Son of God.

Action of the Church at St. Louis, on the death of the Rev. JOHN C. THOM.

At a regular convened meeting of the Congregation of Pine Street Presbyterian Church, on January 2d, 1866, the following preamble and resolutions were unanimously adopted:

In the mysterious providence of God, we are called to mourn the death of Rev. J. C. Thom, pastor elect of this church, who was removed from us on the 28th day of November, 1865.

In view of this unexpected affliction, it becomes us to express our sense of the great loss we have sustained, and our recognition of the Almighty's hand in His strange dealings with our church, already so sorely tried.

When, after a long season of suffering and calamity, Brother Thom came among us to minister to our spiritual wants, we hailed his arrival as the dawn of a brighter day for our dejected and scattered people. We fondly hoped that with the blessing of God attending his prudent and conciliatory conduct, his fervent piety, and his eminent pulpit talents, that he would soon build up our waste places, and refresh our thirsty spirits with the "stream that maketh glad the city of God." But alas! after preaching to us only four Sabbaths, the summons came, which called him from the labors of earth to the rest of heaven.

We are thus again left as a flock without a shepherd, and with earnest entreaty lift up our cry to the Great Head of the Church, for the guidance of His Spirit, and for the abundant communications of His grace in the darkness of this sad dispensation.

Therefore, be it *Resolved*,

First. That as a church we deserve the correction we have received from our heavenly Father, and while submitting to His will, we fervently pray that the chastening may work out the peaceable fruits of righteousness to all the members of this communion.

Second. Feeling that the Lord has a controversy with us, because of our many sins, and especially because of the dissensions and strifes which have rent the bosom of the church, we would humble ourselves in His Holy presence; and joining hands and hearts over the grave of our departed pastor, pledge ourselves, if it be possible, as much as lieth in us to live peaceably with all men, and henceforth to work together in harmony and brotherly love for the advancement of the Redeemer's kingdom.

Third. Our gratitude is due to Almighty God for the deep interest which our deceased brother felt in our welfare, and for the loving supplications which ascended even from his dying bed in our behalf.

Fourth. We desire to express our profound sympathy with his bereaved widow, and fatherless children, and most tenderly commend them to the grace of the compassionate Saviour, who has said, "I will never leave thee nor forsake thee."

Rev. JAMES H. BROOKES, D. D.,
Moderator.

JAMES McQ. DOUGLAS, *Secretary.*

St. Louis, January 2d, 1866.

Resolutions of the Presbytery of Donegal on the death of the Rev. JOHN C. THOM. *April* 12, 1866.

Whereas, This Presbytery has learned that the Rev. John C. Thom has departed this life, since its last meeting, and although not a member of this Presbytery at the time of his decease, yet so short a time having elapsed from leaving us, until he was called away, we consider it appropriate for us, as a Presbytery, to take notice of the death of one who for six years was a member of our body; and

Whereas, While a member of this Presbytery he endeared himself to us by his courteous, obliging, and benevolent demeanor, his uprightness and consistency, his diligence in attendance, and in the performance of all the duties required of him, his zeal for our Master, and his love to all our Master's followers; and

Whereas, We recognize in our deceased brother one well qualified by natural gifts, by education, and by the graces of the Holy Spirit, for the work of the ministry; and do now recognize in his death, though we believe it was gain to him, a great loss to ourselves, his family, the church to which he for a short time ministered, and to the whole church; therefore, be it

Resolved, That we tender our sympathy to his sadly bereaved family; and as our covenant God is faithful, and has promised to be the God of his people and their seed, we trust and pray that our Father in heaven will be a husband to the widow, and a father to the fatherless.

Resolved, That the church to which our deceased brother was called to minister, and which was so soon deprived of one who, by the blessing of God on his labors, was so eminently fitted to build them up in faith, holiness, and peace, and heal all their divisions, has our sincere sympathy in their bereavement, and that our prayer is, that the great Head of the Church may soon give them a pastor to succeed him whom he has so suddenly removed from among them.

Resolved, That copies of these resolutions be sent for publication to the *Presbyterian* and *Presbyterian Banner;* and also to the widow of the deceased.

JOHN FARQUHAR,
Stated Clerk of Presbytery of Donegal.

www.ingramcontent.com/pod-product-compliance
Lightning Source LLC
Chambersburg PA
CBHW032110230426
43672CB00009B/1694